Introduction

A s a chiropractor, I've always known that my body was important for my business. After all, I'm in a physical branch of the healing arts. People pay me to help them feel better in their own bodies. If my body is a mess, then why would they come to me?

But this was just a surface understanding.

When I graduated from chiropractic school, I was just 24 years old. I was so eager to get out and start practicing that I had taken extra classes - even over the summer sessions - all the way through undergrad! I was passionate about the philosophy of chiropractic. I also had the invincible naïveté of a 24-year-old. I thought that everything I needed could be found in books, and that if I just got adjusted regularly, that I would be healthy and successful forever.

Turns out, life and business are more complicated than that.

It took me a long time to realize that all businesses are basically the same. Broadly speaking, they have the same problems. And so, all businesspeople basically have the same challenges. I thought that my challenges as a self-employed chiropractor were special. I thought that they were unique to me and to those within my profession.

As I grew and matured personally and professionally, I learned a lot from various business and self-help resources. Among the various strategies and tips, there were sometimes admonitions to make sure to exercise and get adequate rest. It made sense. Of course, you'll do better in your business if you have more energy!

But I did not *really* grasp how important my connection to my own body was to the health of my business until around 2006. That is when I joined a practice management program called the Home Run Practice (HRP). Home Run Practice was created by fellow chiropractor Dr. Scott Walker. Dr. Walker is the developer of Neuro Emotional Technique (NET), which is my specialty in practice. He launched the Home Run Practice around 2005 specifically for NET practitioners.

Neuro Emotional Technique practitioners needed extra help to run successful practices. They were miles apart from the old stereotypical rack 'em and crack 'em chiropractic model. Thinking I was unique, I had avoided other practice management and mentorship programs. So when I heard about Dr. Walker's new program, I signed on immediately. I could not wait to learn the secrets of success in the practice of NET! I was about eight years into private practice, and while I had learned a lot, I knew that I still had a long way to go.

I remember arriving on the first day and sitting near the front of the room for once. As Dr. Scott started talking, I had my pen in hand, ready to write down his golden nuggets of wisdom. And right out of the gate, it sounded like he was about to hand us the keys to the kingdom! He was about to reveal how we could become **Master Clinicians**.

"What is the main characteristic of the Master Clinician?" he asked.

I waited as he called on people with raised hands. People seemed to give good answers, but none were what he was looking for. Whatever the answer was, I was confident that I could make it happen for myself. Read more books? Take more classes? Get another degree? Hell yeah – I could do any of it! Whatever he said, I could do it. I sat with my pen poised, ready to record the secret that would launch my practice into the stratosphere. Finally, he revealed the secret.

"The Master Clinician," he said, "is, above all... comfortable in his own skin."

My heart sank and my pen dropped. "I'm fucked."

I knew that everyone else in the room was probably uncomfortable in their own skins, too. Hello, human condition. But I doubted that anyone else was as uncomfortable as I was. People could tell that I was "quirky." The fire engine red hair might have been a giveaway. But they didn't know that I was transgender. I was constantly uncomfortable in my skin.

Well, thanks to the support of my fellow NET doctors – especially the HRP docs – I was able to transition. They helped me to muster the courage to begin the outward journey less than a year later. And surprise-not-surprise, I became more and more comfortable in my own skin. My practice and my income grew. My clinical skills sharpened. I was on my way to becoming a Master Clinician!

This trait – that of being comfortable in one's own skin – is a critical component to mastery and deep satisfaction in all walks of life and in all forms of business. Countless coaches, mentors, authors, and speakers say it in their own ways, but the basic message is always the same. Success is an inside job. Happiness is an inside job. You have to feel it in here before you can experience it out there!

But feeling comfortable in your own skin goes far deeper than the skin. It involves understanding yourself. Having compassion for yourself. Working with - not against – yourself. It involves understanding the influences that are working on you from even beyond this lifetime! No, I'm not talking about woo-woo mystery forces, reincarnation, or any of that. I'm talking about your DNA.

Throughout this book, I refer to the body as being separate from the self. This is in complete opposition to what I really believe, which is that for all intents and purposes, you ARE your body! However, it's very difficult to think in these terms because of how our minds perceive reality.

The mind can understand that you have a body. Unless there is pathology present, it knows that your body is your body (as opposed to someone else's). Yet it feels somehow separate – superior in many ways. This is especially true when the body seems to do things on its own volition. Or when it does embarrassing things that the thinking brain would rather it not. Since it is the thinking brain that is reading this book, I will continue to speak of the body as if it were separate. But again, the truth is, you are your body. If that sounds overly simplistic, then you just don't know how complicated, influential, and incredible your body really is!

Everyone wants to make a difference in the world. Everybody wants to leave something worthwhile for the next generation. It is my hope that this book will contribute to the world of mindbody health and the shift towards life balance. Just as "mind" and "body" health are not really separate, so it is that "work" and "life" are not really separate, either. People often talk about the desire for "work-life balance." Isn't that really a search for life balance? Work is a part of life, but life is the whole picture.

As my old Religious Science minister, Dr. J. Kennedy Shulz, used to say, "You are not a birth certificate waiting to become a death certificate." Life is all about what happens in between, and the lead character in that show is your body! Get comfortable in there and enjoy the ride.

CHAPTER 1

Uncomfortable

Most people are not comfortable in their own skin. It's like they're frenemies with their own bodies.

My own adversarial relationship with my body began at a very young age. I hesitate to even share this first memory because, frankly, it is so embarrassing. I'm sure it's happened to countless people, although most are fortunate enough to have no memory of it.

My very first memory ever comes from when I was just a baby. I don't know how old I was, but small enough to be in diapers and unable to speak. I remember feeling perfectly content at first. Happy, just enjoying life, looking around. I was with my dad in the little apartment on Glebe Road – 333 Glebe Road – Dominion Arms, in Arlington, Virginia. I remember my dad laying me down on the floor of the small bathroom (which, to me, looked huge) and getting ready to change my diaper. Even though I was a baby, I felt a sense of nervousness. Even though I couldn't control it yet, I knew that I was about to shit, and that it was going to be a big one. I had no way of communicating this to my dad. So I just lay there kicking my little legs and hoping for the best.

What followed was even worse than I had imagined.

It wasn't just a big poop. It was explosive diarrhea. From my baby perspective, it looked as if the entire room had been sprayed with crap! My dad, a neurotic clean freak, was covered in baby diarrhea. He started yelling and gesturing around, flailing arms, red face twisted up with disgust, and as for me?

I wanted to die.

I could feel my own face turning red and I started WAILING.

The louder my dad yelled, the louder I cried and screamed, too, and probably kept pooping as well. Who knows how long this screaming poop fest went on? I don't think my dad hit me or anything like that – he was not really the hitter in the family – but the deep sense of shame was hard to shake.

My body had betrayed me.

It did a really stupid thing that made my dad really really mad and it embarrassed the hell out of me.

My body could not be trusted.

As I got older, my body betrayed me in yet more ways. In school, I discovered that I was a stutterer. I didn't stutter on all words – only on certain sounds. The most inconvenient sounds! How can a sound be inconvenient? When the sounds that you stutter on are the "K" and "M" sounds and both your first and last name contain BOTH of those sounds. That's inconvenient!

The first day of school was always dreadful. The very first time I would have to speak was always to say my own name and correct the teacher on the pronunciation. As you can see from the cover, my name is Kim Makoi. But I changed the spelling of my last name way back in 1999. It was pronounced the same, but was spelled McCaughey.

So, on the first day of school, the teacher would call roll and say, "Kimberly... Mc... McCoffee? Mc...Mc-Cay-hey? How do you say your name?"

And I would have to stand up, gulp a bunch of air, breathe, wait, and spit it out.

"M-m-m-m...Mcc-c-c-c...McCoy."

Mortifying. I hated it.

Even before considering a gender-related name change, I always knew that I wanted to change my last name. At least change the spelling of it so that people would stop asking me to pronounce it.

I also hated the inevitable follow-up question.

"You don't look Irish. Where are you from?"

I knew what they were asking, but I was a sassy kid, and I would always look at them and say, "I'm from Washington, DC." Which is where I was born. Now, I have a made-up ambiguously Asian-looking name. I'm an ambiguously Asian-looking person, so nobody asks anymore! It makes it extra funny, too, when I receive spam e-mails about a wealthy "distant relative" with the last name Makoi whose estate has been searching for me, the sole heir! Yeah... if only!

The stuttering forced me to become creative when it came to conversations and asking or answering questions in school. I was always trying to figure out how to ask or say things without having to make a K or an M sound in the beginning of a sentence!

For example, whenever I needed to ask to go to the bathroom, I could never ask, "Can I go to the bathroom?" because I would stutter on the C. So, I would always say, "It is OK if I go to the bathroom?"

The stuttering thing might also be why I was so excited at age 7 to discover that there is a thing called a pen-pal. A friend that you never have to speak to! You just write to them!

I remember around 1980 or 1981, during Saturday morning cartoons, there was an ad for Dear Pen Pal. It featured a cartoon globe spinning around, sending and receiving letters. I still remember the address where you could send away for a pen-pal! It was Dear Pen Pal, PO Box 4054 Santa Barbara, CA 93103. The commercial ended with a sing-songy "Sure you've lots to say!" I can't remember how many pen-pals I sent away for, but I am still in touch with two of them!

More body disasters? Well, I was always the weak kid. As a January baby, I was on the older side of the kids in my grade, and I was one of the tallest kids – almost always the tallest girl. Yes, even as a little kid, people would ask dumb things like if I was interested in basketball. No, I'm not. I'm interested in books.

The expectation was always that I would be a fast runner or otherwise good in sports. I was neither. I was always the slowest or 2nd slowest kid in the whole class. I remember the elementary school P.E. teacher, Mr. Fiddler, always looking at me with disdain and asking why I didn't just try harder. I really was trying! But I could never even win one of those "Standard" level merit badges they used to give out back then!

I was always the last to get picked for kickball and that sort of thing. Once, in 6th grade, I remember it came down to me and a kid named Andrew. The team captains kept looking back and forth at me, and Andrew, me, Andrew, me, Andrew... Who was truly the worst kid to pick last?

Finally, one captain said, "You can just have Kim AND Andrew." And the other captain was like, "No, YOU can have Kim AND Andrew." And they were literally arguing over who should take us BOTH. It was awful.

And then there's the gender stuff. I knew by age 4 that I was transgender, but I had no idea there was a word for it until I was 18! It didn't help that often, noting my ineptitude in the kitchen, my mom would say things like, "You should have been born a boy." Yeah, no shit, lady!

When I looked in the mirror, I didn't connect with the body I saw. I hated it and I wished that I could function as just a mind. Was there a job where you could get paid to read books and write letters? Because that sounded like a good job to me. (I never realized until way too late that apparently, lawyers are basically paid to read and write!)

I also had frequent headaches from a very young age. They happened regularly at least once a month but usually more often. I remember complaining about it to my parents when I was around 8 years old and my dad chimed in, "Maybe it's that time of the month!" and I was like, "DAD! I'm 8!!!" I barely knew what a period was, but I thought that as an adult, HE should know! The headaches also felt like a betrayal. The weakness, the headaches, the runny nose.

Why was my body so lame?

I made my way through childhood basically as a brain. I got good grades, made friends through the pen-pal system and later through computer Bulletin Board Systems (BBSes). I'm still friends with a lot of my BBS friends today! As far as I was concerned, my body could fuck off and die. It didn't affect my life much and I was positive that it didn't affect my brain or my success!

Turns out, I was wrong.

The gender thing has been a long journey indeed. As I'm writing this, I'm in my bearded middle aged bald guy phase of life. It's funny, as much as I never wanted to be a soft-bellied bald guy, I don't feel uncomfortable at all when I look at myself in the mirror.

I just think, yep, there I am.

Whereas the whole time of my life living as a female, I would always squint at myself in the mirror. I would squint and try to see if I could see the real me – the male me. I never squint anymore. Nevertheless, even though I feel basically good about my body now, the gender thing still messes with me.

I'm probably known for my signature spine and skeleton tuxedo t-shirts, which have become my uniform over the years. I love these t-shirts! They bring me and others a lot of joy. Though, I do get that it can be creepy at times.

I once had an OKCupid profile, which I decided to take a closer look at one day. Upon inspection, I realized that in all seven of the pictures I'd posted – from various events and different years – I was wearing the same shirt! They all featured me wearing the exact same skeleton t-shirt! (Thank you skeletees.com for keeping me in fresh skeleton t-shirts for 22+ years!)

I could see that this was a little crazy. It might have been off-putting or frightening to someone. But hey, if they're not comfortable with that t-shirt, then dating me was going to be a problem. So, I left it.

While I genuinely do love that t-shirt – some of them even glow in the dark! – the fact is, it's a fantastic shirt for hiding the female chest. People either didn't notice or perhaps just pitied me for my man boobs. But the self-consciousness about the chest was part of what kept me from wearing more traditional work shirts. (note: I finally got my chest surgery during the editing of this book! The fate of the spine t-shirt remains to be seen.)

But the most traumatizing and unforgiveable body betrayal of my life came with pregnancy and childbirth. Pregnancy started out OK, but it was a bit of a mindfuck. I was already transgender identified and wearing only men's clothing. It was incredibly upsetting when I had to start wearing women's underwear. Maternity underwear, because the men's underwear did not work anymore on my pregnant body!

And the chest changes. Oh my gawd. My breasts got huge. After giving birth as the milk was coming in, they ballooned from an A to a massive G cup size! They were rock hard and full of milk. I thought, whoa, this is what they mean when they call them "jugs" and "melons." They felt as hard and heavy as watermelons!

NOT SEXY!

They were painful, and while they looked cool – if you're into boobs – they were painful and mortifying to me. And... they leaked! I had to wear BOOB PADS to prevents giant embarrassing milk leaks all over my shirt at random times! It was AWFUL awful awful. Eventually, the monster tits subsided, but then I was left with little saggy boobs that could not pass either for man boobs.

And that was just the part that I could talk about. I couldn't speak to anyone – not even a therapist – about the trauma of what was going on down below.

I wanted to die.

I was so disconnected from my body, I felt like a zombie – a walking dead person – for at least two years, probably three years after my son was born. I felt horrible at the time and still do about what he probably lacked in terms of motherly nourishing during that critical time. I did my best as I went through the motions of life, but emotionally and physically I felt awful.

More than ever, I thought, FUCK THIS BODY. WHO NEEDS A BODY? I wish I were just a brain!

I'm not sure how I would have gotten through that time if I hadn't been in a job where I had to help other people to feel comfortable in *their* bodies! In many ways, my profession has saved me and helped me to make friends with my body at last.

It's a long story.

How did someone who hates needing a body end up becoming a chiropractor?

I never meant to become one. I didn't even know what they did until I was 18.

Growing up, I always dreamed of going to the U.S. Naval Academy and following in my grandfather's footsteps. I wanted to become an officer in the U.S. Navy, and not just any officer. I dreamed of becoming the first female admiral ever!

My grandfather smiled through gritted teeth when I told him this. Truth be told, it probably made his stomach turn. I didn't know that one of the reasons he retired from the Navy when he did was because the Navy had started to admit women. My grandfather was like, I will have no part of this organization if there are going to be women in the ranks! Fooey!

So he retired as a Captain and started a new career as an L.A. harbor pilot. He worked until he got sick with lung cancer, which may have been a result of his years on a submarine. Back then, they used a lot of asbestos in submarines. He died on Bill Clinton's inauguration day, which was funny. Grandpa used to always pound his fists on the breakfast table and yell things like, "A Democrat in the White House? Over my dead body!"

My Navy dreams came to a crashing halt once I realized that I would have cut my hair and *exercise* to join!

No way was I going to cut my hair, and HELL NO WAY was I going to exercise! I was going to quit P.E. as soon as possible. Only 2 years of Physical Education were required to graduate from high school. And then? I was never going to exercise again for the rest of my life!

If only I had a time machine, I could go back and smack myself across the face and be like, "Dude! I'm here to tell you that you are going to be a bald middle-aged guy who ends up having to exercise! Get over it, go to the Naval Academy, get a good free education, and have a nice pension someday! Jeez-us!"

Honestly, I didn't have much interest in becoming a doctor, but I was trying to make my mom happy. Mom had a "people like us don't make it" philosophy. She explained that "people like us" have no wealth or special social connections needed to get the cushy or "soft" jobs in life, such as those in the liberal arts. According to mom, there were only three career paths for "people like us." We could become soldiers, priests or doctors.

If I had been born as a boy in the first place, I would have probably chosen the path of priest-monk. I would have disappeared to a solitary Russian Orthodox monastery somewhere in Alaska. Ah yes, reading books, thinking a lot, and probably not exercising. (Although, now that I know more about what real life in isolated places actually entails, I'm sure that those monks do indeed get plenty of exercise!)

But the life of a nun did not appeal to me at all, and the military was out due to my aversion to haircuts and exercise. That left me with pre-med. Besides, the pre-med pathway was also my ticket out of northern Virginia. I could get to California with an academic scholarship. I could get to my dream city of San Francisco by securing said scholarship at the University of San Francisco. USF is a Jesuit school, which was the only kind of school that my Catholic parents would agree to let me run off to!

The day before leaving for California, Fate knocked on my front door in the form of a young chiropractor named Andrew Smith. He was going door-to-door meeting neighbors and marketing his new practice. "Hi, neighbor! I'm the new chiropractor in town, and I'm meeting neighbors to see what they think about chiropractic."

"Well," I said, "I'm not going to be your neighbor after today, so you don't need to meet me."

"Oh," he said," that's too bad, where are you moving to?"

"San Francisco!" I proudly proclaimed.

"Really?" he said, "I just came from San Francisco! I went to chiropractic school in Hayward, right near San Francisco. Why are you moving to San Francisco?"

"To go to pre-med at USF."

"Pre-med?" he said, " you don't want to be a medical doctor! You want to be a chiropractor!"

"I don't want to be a chiropractor," I said, "I don't want to be a back doctor."

"Back doctor??" he seemed insulted. "Do you have a minute??"

So I let him tell me about chiropractic. He told me that chiropractic school and medical school are basically the same thing for the first two years. Then, medical students start learning about drugs and surgery. Chiropractic students learn about technique, x-ray and nutrition. They learn about how to get people well without drugs and surgery.

He had charts and brochures that showed me the differences between medical and chiropractic education. He showed me his spinal charts showing how the nerves to the spine connected to every muscle and organ the body. He told me that spinal health affects not just back pain but everything in the body!

He planted a seed in my mind that I had never expected. I wasn't about to change my career path based on a single conversation with a random chiropractor knocking on my door, but I was intrigued. As pre-med wore on, I realized that I was not that interested in drugs, surgery or hospitals. I couldn't relate to my fellow pre-med students. Being a young self-employed chiropractor, working in my own private practice, with my own two hands on my own terms sounded better and better to me.

I could be working on my own as early as age 24 if I plowed through school at breakneck speed.

That sounded great!

After just a year of pre-med, I decided to change course and started my chiropractic prerequisites. I enrolled in Life Chiropractic College in Marietta, Georgia, in January of 1994.

I thought that I had chosen the perfect profession.

There would be no crisis, save for losing my hands, through which I would not be able to keep working. Old chiropractors told stories of how their old mentors had managed to thrive even during The Great Depression. Back then, they sometimes bartered chiropractic for chickens!

I figured that even if I had somehow been wrongfully jailed - an irrational fear I'd has since childhood – I would still be OK. I could barter chiropractic adjustments for protection and goods! If I were randomly dropped in a random location anywhere in the world, I could still somehow eke out a living as long as there were people with spines! I was confident that I had the ultimate in job security!

Until the spring of 2020.

Well, the pandemic was a bit of a shocker. While everyone was "working from home" and pivoting, I got lost in a funk. I felt like my life had been like a Choose Your Own Adventure book, and I had made the wrong choice and found myself facing an early and embarrassing demise.

I treated my body badly, eating way too much Trader Joe's mochi ice cream, and I quickly gained my own "covid 19" as they say. I slowly pulled myself together as the year wore on, and business started to pick up again, but my body was not doing so great.

Various stressors had accumulated over the last couple of years and I had dropped my self-care routines. I hadn't gotten adjusted in a while. I stopped my daily beach walks when MUNI stopped the trains in May. My blood sugar was a mess, and I should have known – but didn't – that I was a disaster waiting to happen.

Disaster struck quietly on Tuesday March 3, 2021, at around 11am. I had just finished seeing a patient, when I felt like I was having a low blood sugar attack. I felt a bit weak, and it felt like my heart was starting to race faster. So I went upstairs, ate some soup and had a few almonds. The weak feeling and the fluttery heart beats didn't improve.

In fact, it felt worse. And worse.

I thought to myself, "Huh... this... feels like what atrial fibrillation sounds like..."

As luck (or paranoia) would have it, I did have my own small personal EKG unit. (Shout out to KardiaMobile!)

I ran my own EKG. The graph looked like a mess, and it didn't take an expert to know that something was wrong. The message on the graph spelled out the obvious: "Suspected atrial fibrillation. Consult with your doctor."

Instead of calling my doctor, of course, I Googled, "Do you need to go to the hospital for atrial fibrillation?"

Yes. The answer was yes.

After dragging my ass, calling Kaiser and confirming that I should go to the hospital, I waited for my partner to come over and drive me to the ER.

From my (one) experience, the real-life ER is nothing like the TV and movie ER. It's actually a rather quiet place and everyone seems pretty chill. I wonder if this is because they are trained to keep the patients calm and not trigger bigger and badder heart attacks and all that!

There's nothing quite like sitting in the ER with a bunch of wires coming off your chest to get you thinking.

While sitting there, I thought about how short my life could be. How I might not even make it to 50, much less 75, 80 or beyond. Well, that changed my perspective real fast. It lit a fire under my ass to finally focus like a laser and do my very best most specialized work for the rest of my career.

I vowed to quit wasting time futzing around as a generalist. I had been doing excellent work for some people, good work for a lot of people and unimpressive work for a few people.

As I thought about my mortality, I realized that I didn't have any of the typical regrets of the dying (more on that later). But I did have one big regret, which was that I had not passed the baton. I did not pass on the knowledge that I had gained throughout my life and career in any lasting way.

My website and blog would likely vanish as soon as the automatic payments lapsed. My social media footprints are woefully devoid of the most beneficial knowledge that I have to share! And so this book came into being following my kind-of-sort-of-near-death-experience. Call it "near death lite."

The atrial fibrillation event was a big wake-up call for me.

Do I want to live? Do I still have work to do? Yes and yes.

I could not afford to be enemies with my body. We had to join forces and make it work!

Shit just got real.

Chapter 2

Stop Hitting Yourself

There is a great meme that makes the rounds every so often in some of my social media circles. It shows a famous engraving by the artist Gustave Doré. It's called Jacob Wresting with the Angel. In the meme, there is a quote over the image that usually says something like this:

"And the angel said unto him, 'Stop hitting yourself. Stop hitting yourself.' But lo, he could not. For the angel was hitting him with his own hands."

This meme makes me laugh every time!

I love it.

Why do I love it so much?! I love it because it captures so much of the struggle. We want to be good, and we want to align with our highest and best! But sometimes it feels like we're at war with our own self. And what's worse, it can feel like our own self is the schoolyard bully, grabbing our own hands and hitting us with them, and then taunting us. Stop hitting yourself! Stop hitting yourself!

Why do we do that? Because we hate ourselves? Because we're "afraid of success?"

No. It's because we don't know what our own brain has concluded about our world and how it's been programmed to operate within it.

How can we not know our own brain? How did we come to be at such odds with our own bodies? It seems like we are the only animals in the world that need a whole lifetime to figure out how to live a life!

Unfortunately, the part of your brain that does the thinking is not the part of the brain that controls, well, much of anything. There are some sophisticated models of how the brain works, but I'm going to use a simplified one that we'll call The Three Brains model.

The brain can generally be broken down into three main parts. These three parts are both structurally and functionally different. They are the reptilian brain, the mammalian brain and the neocortex.

The deepest part of the brain is the reptilian brain. It's almost identical to the brain that is found in reptiles. This brain all about surviving and responding to danger. It's the four Fs: fight, flight, food and reproduction. This brain is always looking at things and thinking, "Should I eat it? Should I fight it? Should I fuck it? Should I run away?"

It's where instinct and genetically programmed behaviors live. It controls the basics of life: breathing, heart rate, primitive muscle reflexes and sensations. It's about aggression, territoriality and dominance. Posturally, it's dominant in the lying down position. When someone is alive but brain dead or in a coma, this is the part of the brain that is still working. There's no thinking and logic happening here. It's mostly unconscious and is difficult to access directly. Since this is the brain that keeps you alive, it has a ton of control.

The reptile brain takes over when life and death are at stake. I have had at least two memorable experiences with coming face to face with my own reptile brain! I consider myself to be a very chill person, peaceful and maybe even a bit wimpy. I'm never looking for a fight, that's for sure! I'm afraid of tall people and of giant cockroaches! I always figured that I would be really afraid if I ever came close to dying.

When I was around 16 or 17, I narrowly missed being in what I felt certain would be a fatal high-speed car accident on the highway. Time slowed down, and as the car slid toward impact with the other car, I felt a strong emotion – not fear, but ANGER rising in my body! I felt a burning hot rage while simultaneously feeling an energy that started at the tip of my toes and rose up through my body. I don't know what it was, but it felt like my soul itself was about to leave my body and that it would pop right out the top of my head! But as the crazy energy went up to my throat, the car avoided the impact and miraculously righted itself on the road!

Death and disaster averted!

My soul (or whatever) stopped the ascent, but not before it moved just a little further up, to my mouth, where for a second, I could taste it! It was a salty bitter taste. That's what my soul tastes like, I guess – salty and bitter! Seems legit. Anyway, I had never come that close to death before, and it was not what I expected.

The other time my reptile brain very much surprised me was the time that I found a man hiding in the janitor closet at my office one evening. I was headed there to leave the recycling and to wash a few dishes. I was the only person in the office. Everyone else had left for the night. So I stepped into the closet and looked to my right. Just about 2 feet away from me stood an unexpected stranger!

If you had asked me how I thought I would react hypothetically in a situation like that, I would have thought that I would expect to be startled and afraid. I'm not a fighter and I also hate confrontations. I would have had to play it tough or play it cool or something.

But how did I feel when the encounter really happened? It felt like a switch flipped inside of my brain and like a totally different persona took over.

I wasn't afraid at all. I wasn't angry, either. The weird feeling that came over me was... excitement! I felt excited, and my brain was like, "Oh! Do we get to kill it?" I know, I know, that sounds really bad. I swear, I'm not a killer – I can't even kill mice!

But in that potential life/death moment, my reptile brain kicked in.

More than likely, so did the DNA memory of my killer ancestors who had to survive in the brutal world that was most of human history! I don't know if the stranger standing in the closet could sense the creepy killer DNA awakening within me, but he put his hands up in defense and muttered something about how he didn't mean any harm and that he was just leaving!

I have a prison pen-pal who told a similar tale of being overcome by the survival brain. A few years into his sentence, he was caught in the middle of a prison riot. My friend, despite being in prison, was not a violent offender, and was never what you'd call a fighter. He was an artist who wrote letters with bubble-shaped cursive handwriting that looked like it belonged to a 9-year-old girl. (Although these days, 9-year-old girls don't even know how to read cursive, much less write in it anymore.)

At some point during the riot, he felt something stab him in the leg. His memory is not clear about what happened next or how the riot ended, but at the end of it, he got out with just the one stab in the leg. But apparently, during the fuzzy memory part, he had grabbed the shiv and stabbed the other guy with it 24 times!

That there was pure reptile brain in action.

Unfortunately for my friend, while it may have been self-defense, they still added about ten years onto his sentence for it.

Side note: you may be wondering why I have prison pen-pals. I just enjoy writing letters. These days, most people do e-mail, text, etc. In the old days, it was easy to find good old-fashioned pen-pals! Now, the only people stuck with writing letters seem to be prisoners. I picked a few addresses out of the Black and Pink pen-pal newsletter and made some new friends. Black and Pink (www.blackandpinkpenpals.org) is an organization that connects incarcerated LGBTQ+ people with pen-pals. While most of my prison pen-pals are indeed

LGBTQ+, I discovered that a fair number of straight people add their name to the list because they are so desperate for pen-pals!

One guy I wrote to had been in for almost 20 years, and he hadn't received a single piece of mail in more than a decade! Cynical people will say that nothing good could possibly come from writing to people who are in prison, but I say that's not true. Having prison pen-pals gives you a whole new perspective on the prison system, on "criminals" and on humanity. OK - back to the book.

The next layer of brain to evolve, which is really the largest part of the brain, is called the mammalian brain. All mammals share this brain structure. This is the part of the brain that controls more complicated physiological functions. These include hormones, temperature control, complex sensations and perceptions, memory formation and emotions. Sexuality is also found here. We're talking about the variations and nuances, as opposed to just the straight up reproductive sex act.

The mammalian brain is relationship oriented (good or bad, friends or enemies) and perfectionistic. It is timeless. Everything that has ever happened is happening at once in the mammalian brain. This is why when you are deep in a heavy emotional state, time seems to vanish. On one extreme, you can fall in love, feel an incredible connection to someone, and think, "Wow, it feels like I've known you FOREVER!" and on the other side of the coin, you can have a terrible break up with someone, or experience betrayal and think. "I'll NEVER love or trust again!"

Logic does not rule here.

Interestingly, the mammalian brain is also where we find religious tendencies and altruism. We generally don't think of other mammals as having spirituality, but really, how would we know? I read that elephants have been seen performing what sure look like rudimentary religious activities. Things like waving tree branches at the full moon or ritual bathing under the full moon.

The mammalian brain also has a hard time telling real from imagined.

Try this. Imagine that you are holding a big juicy lemon. You know it's a juicy one because it feels heavy in your hand. Now, take that lemon and slice it into big wedges. Smell the lemony goodness. You were right about the juiciness, because the juice is all over your hands now. Dry off your hands with a paper towel, and while you're at it, take the dry part of the paper towel and pat your tongue with it! Because why not? Now, lift a lemon wedge up to your mouth and take a big bite. Chew it up good!

If you imagined it hard enough, then you likely experienced a salivary response. Your body reacted to an idea as if it were real! It's getting ready to digest that lemon!

This is also why your heart speeds up and your palms get sweaty while you're watching a scary movie. You know it's fake, but there's a part of your brain that can't tell the difference. So, your body starts to get ready to run away or fight!

The mammalian brain is mostly subconscious, so we're not that aware of what's happening there, but it's easier to access than the reptilian brain. Posturally, this brain is easiest to access when we're in the quadripedic position, or on our hands and knees.

The latest part of the brain to evolve is the neocortex. This part of the brain is mostly conscious. This is the part that does the thinking, talking, math, etc. This is the part of the brain where we are having that annoying inner dialogue with ourselves! This is the brain that thinks it's in charge.

It's not.

In fact, it's the last to find out about anything!

There is a fascinating area of neurophilosophy that concerns itself with the neuroscience of free will. A famous study in the 1980s by Benjamin Libet suggested that the conscious "will" to do something was preceded – by as much as half a second – by a subconscious impulse that the study participant was completely unaware of. While his study and methods have been criticized over the years, and the half second time window may have been exaggerated due to the study design, the basic premise has held. Subconscious processes largely drive action.

More often than not, when say that we decided to do a thing, we are making up a story about something that the body was already doing. On the far extreme, some neuroscientists now believe that there is no such thing as free will. They believe that we are just reacting off of reflexes – a complex series of stimulus/response.

It reminds me of a dinner party where I met a couple of scientists who were married to each other. They said that before having a kid, they debated a lot on the nature/nurture thing. They concluded that nurture has to be stronger than nature when it came to raising a child. They were confident that when they became parents, they would be able to shape their little one into the person they wanted them to be.

Their child had not even hit the 2-year-old mark when they both concluded that they were wrong. It's pretty much all nature. Nurture barely makes any difference at all.

They felt like idiots.

I believe that the truth is somewhere in between.

When I say "in between," I don't mean 50/50. I believe that the nature side outweighs the nurture side considerably. I believe that we DO have more power to influence our outcomes than we think, even if nature is stronger than nurture.

But the only way to do this is to work **with** our natures, and not against them. The animal brains always win because survival always wins. The human thinking brain, with all its language and philosophy, was the last one to the show up and it has the least rank and clout.

So, if we take the three brains analogy another step, think of it like this. Imagine that you have, living inside of you, a reptile, a non-human mammal – say, a cat – and then the human that you identify as "me."

You're having a hard time. You decide that you're not going to eat ice cream for dinner anymore. You write a shopping list, you head to the store, and you vow, NO ICE CREAM. We're NOT doing that anymore. We're going to buy kale, yogurt, maybe some granola if we're going to go crazy, but NO ICE CREAM for dinner! Nyet!

And then you're wandering around the store, filling up your basket. You reach the ice cream aisle. Instead of skipping the aisle all together, you turn into it.

"Just to see."

And somehow, mysteriously, your arm reaches out, opens the cooler door, and pulls out a delicious little pint of Rocky Road. Isn't there a holiday next week? Yeah, a holiday! So it's basically a special occasion. Grab a vanilla while you're at it. I mean, like, vanilla is so boring. Does it even count as ice cream? It's practically diet food. Oh! Hey! If we get that "keto" ice cream, doesn't that almost make it, like a vegetable? Close enough!

You get home, look in the freezer, and feel ashamed. Who did that? Who bought that? We weren't going to get any ice cream. Well, start again tomorrow. Or next week.

The real problem is, that person who decided to stop buying ice cream is not the person in control. Those other fellas inhabiting your body – the snake and the cat – didn't get the memo.

It's not that they heard you but are rebelling like sullen teens.

They didn't hear you.

They might have heard you in the way that we hear the adults in Charlie Brown cartoons – speaking like, wah wah wha, wa wahhh wah. Complete gibberish. You may as well have been mumbling about the propositions on the upcoming state election ballot! Blah blah blah blah blah.

Instead, what happened was, those animals are living in a magical world. A world where they can drive cars and use money. And you essentially handed them your wallet and keys and let them loose in a food heaven.

What do you think they were going to do?

They're going to get the thing that they are pulled to get, unless they are compelled by some stronger force to do otherwise.

Can you do a thing by sheer force of will? Yes, you can.

This is kind of like keeping your pet on a leash. The pet may not like it – especially the cat! – but it can be done. But that does take conscious effort and discipline. Ideally, you want to develop positive habits so that things run on the good kind of autopilot.

To be honest most people are asleep at the wheel. They have no conscious awareness about what is going on.

Or their role in it.

Or the fact that they can change it - if only they make the commitment to FOCUS and DO THE THING!

And if they can't do the thing, then they need the wherewithal to be able to take a step back and say, "OK, I can't seem to do this alone. I'm going to reach out for help."

And now, we're off to the races!

In a lot of ways, you are your own hostage. You're trapped in a prison of your own making. In patterns that you have been stuck with for so long you might not even be able to remember what "freedom" felt like.

You can't get out!

The hostage takers won't let you go because they have demands.

You need to keep the shitty job because if you leave then you might lose your home. You might get kicked out on the streets. Then what? You better just stay in that job that you hate.

You can't leave the shitty relationship because who will ever love you and where will you go? You better stay because the devil you know is better than the devil you don't!

You seem doomed to continue to repeat the same unhealthy patterns. In relationship, finance, business, friendships... why? Because the survival brain knows that you know how to survive these things! It doesn't care about whether you are "happy" or not. To be honest, it's not worth the risk!

Millions of years of evolution of life on earth have really nailed it deep into the programming that the prime directive is SURVIVAL. If you can survive something, GREAT. Want to try something new? Not so much. Too risky.

But there are ways to appease the body hostage takers and to win your freedom. Their demands seem unreasonable, but they're not. Ultimately, what they want is food, safety, security and probably some sex. Again, remember, the reptile brain is about the 4 Fs.

Chapter 3

Good S.E.C.S.

Winning your release from the body hostage takers is simple, but it's hard work. Freedom sounds so sexy, but the road to get there is not. That's why I decided to give it the acronym S.E.C.S. – because you want good S.E.C.S.! You're welcome, and I'm sorry. Good S.E.C.S. means that you've got to cover Structure, Emotions, Chemistry and Spirituality*. I put the * next to the Spirituality because I don't equate spirituality with religion. I don't even equate it with the belief in a God or any other entity. Atheists can have a rich spiritual life – even without a belief in "spirits." More on that later.

Now, here's the weird thing about the body. Sometimes – and for some people all of the time – it doesn't make sense. It's hard to understand how doing something to, for or with the body will have a direct impact on something like your mental state or your business or your life trajectory. It often won't make any sense until *after* the fact! That's just the way it is. It seems like a bug in the program, but more than likely, it's a feature. When it comes to the body, do the thing first, observe, and then come to your conclusions later. Remember, the neocortex, or the thinking brain, is the last to know!

Structure

Structural health is important! Structure determines function. Can we agree on that?

Anything with any kind of structure has evolved that way for a specific reason. If we neglect the structure, then things will tend to malfunction and break down.

Have you ever stubbed a little toe or broken a toe or had a cut on a little toe? Isn't it shocking how such a tiny injury to a tiny part of the body can have a huge impact on how you are able to move through your day? The human body is incredibly interconnected.

You would think that the structural health of your body would not have much to do with the health of your business. That is, unless you are in a physically demanding job. If you are a manual laborer, then of course you will need a strong back and shoulders. If you are a dancer, then of course you will need optimal structural integrity!

But what about if you are an entrepreneur? Or a graphic designer?

The structural integrity of your body still affects your livelihood in many ways. Your body is how you move through the world. It's the lens through which you perceive the world. And it's also a big part of how people perceive you.

Let's say you're on vacation in a beautiful location. You're on the Big Island – Hawaii! You are in bliss. How do you know it's bliss? Because you are relaxing on a soft lounge under the shade of a tree. You can smell the wonderful aroma of the plumerias and other tropical flowers. You can feel a gentle sea breeze against your skin. You can feel the warm touch of the sun as it peeks through the branches. Your muscles are relaxed. There's no tension in your body. Your belly is relaxed, and it moves up and down with the rhythm of your breath. You have a little smile on your face. *This is the life.*

But what happens if the structure is out of whack? You're sitting on that same soft lounge in that same beautiful location, but you're not quite in the bliss. Your jaw is tight and clicking on one side whenever you open your mouth. You can't get comfortable because there's a pinching feeling near the top of your back, just below your neck. Your arms feel tight, and your hand keeps kind of going numb. It feels weaker than it used to. Your hand aches a bit. Your low back is sore, kind of a dull throb. Your hamstrings and calf are a bit crampy even though you didn't do anything. Your belly is tight and kind of bloated, and you can feel a little bit of reflux wanting to kick in. This vacation sucks a little bit.

The feelings of "good" or "bad" times are experienced *through* your body.

How do you think it is when you are showing up in person for clients or business associates?

Do you think it would make a difference, whether you were fully present and feeling solid in your physical body? Do you think it would go better than if you were showing up experiencing uncomfortable imbalances?

Of course, it makes a difference!

When you feel great, you feel great. Everyone prefers to be around other people who are feeling great.

You could spend a lifetime learning to take care of the structure of your body. We are only going to hit some of the highlights here. Posture and movement are the obvious things that come to mind when we think of body structure.

How your body moves can impact your business.

This was one of the most horrifying realizations of all time for me. I don't dance, I don't do karaoke, I don't do sports. I do not like to move my body in front of people. And yet, it's a pretty important component of any kind of social interaction. The body. Or should I say, duh! Body!

You can see it easily in other people, when you notice someone slouched over or someone with terrible posture. There's a feeling that comes with that, and it's not a good one. Your posture not only tells people how you're feeling. It can emphasize certain feelings while de-emphasizing others.

Do this experiment right now. Cross your arms. Slump down in your chair. Hang your head down in sad sack position. Put a frown on your face. Furrow your eyebrows. Breathe shallow. Now, try as hard as you can to think of the greatest day of your whole life! The happiest moment ever! It's almost impossible to really tap into that happy feeling while you are holding your body in that sad posture, right? For me, it's almost impossible to even picture the happy memory! It's crazy.

And now, try the opposite. Sit or stand up straight, shoulders back. Put your hands on your hips in the superhero position, head slightly tilted up, with a big wide smile on your face. Now, try thinking about the saddest day of your life and really try and feel the sad or awful feeling. It's not easy, is it? In fact, it's almost impossible to really feel the fullness of the sadness while the body is in the happy triumphant posture!

Sadly, I have never been a fan of exercise. I was always happy to just read books all day! Exercise? Feh! That was for jocks and jerks. I associated exercise with the humiliating hell that was P.E. class. I vowed that after 10th grade – my final required P.E. credits – that I would never "exercise" again.

Ah, the follies of youth.

Turns out, exercise is important. Our bodies were designed to move, and without regular movement, it deteriorates. Even the mere act of moving around from day to day against gravity serves important functions in the body. It's shocking how quickly astronauts – people who train to be in tip-top physical health – lose bone mass from a short amount of time spent in zero gravity! The body is very much a use-it-or-lose-it apparatus.

Movement is important not just for strength and flexibility, but for immunity and mental acuity as well. The lymphatic system, which is a major part of the immune system does not have an external pump of its own, unlike the circulatory system. It relies instead on muscular contraction. Without adequate muscle activity, the lymph has poor circulation and tends to stagnate. Recent research even shows that movement is an important component of hydration! Through movement, water is transported to tissues all over the body by way of the fascia.

Fascia is a thin connective tissue that holds every muscle, bone, and organ in place. This huge and critical part of the body has been overlooked until just recently. In cadaver dissections, it was already limp and dehydrated, so it never seemed to be anything of consequence. Hand surgeon and author Dr. Jean-Claude Guimberteau was the first person to film living fascia using a special endoscope. His short film, Strolling Under the Skin, shows fascinating images of living fascia! You can check it out on YouTube. This was the first time that fascia was observed as a dynamic tissue with a functional role and not just a structural one.

There is plenty of research that shows that movement and exercise improve almost everything, as far as the health of the body is concerned. Just a few of the things that benefit from exercise include blood sugar, cardiovascular health, memory, anxiety, depression, and cognitive function. Just as we know that we should be eating better than we are, we also know what we should be doing better with exercise. The problem is, we don't want to, and therefore, we don't.

Millions of people buy gym memberships that they never use. I'm not sure that anyone really enjoys "exercise." If people do like to exercise, it's more likely that they like to do something that happens to involve exercise. So then the trick and the challenge is that you (yes, you) have to find *something that you enjoy doing.*

It's no longer up for discussion as to whether exercise is good for you.

It's good for you.

The only question is, what am I going to do that happens to also be exercise? Some people love going to the gym more for the people-watching than for the exercising, but it lights them up and gets them the physical action they need! Some people love to take fitness classes for the group element. It doesn't matter too much *what* you do as long as you are getting full-body activity.

I used to wonder how my parents seemed to remain relatively lean and fit throughout their lives, even though they didn't seem to "exercise." My dad in particular seemed to be always sitting down and reading a book whenever he had the chance.

But as I got older, I realized that boring yard and housework could be physically demanding. I realized that my dad's OCD around keeping the house totally clean created his own weird little gym! He was constantly getting up and down to wipe the floor or reaching up to dust shelves that I was pretty sure nobody could even see.

And mom was doing the same sorts of thing in her huge garden. Getting up and down to do the weeding and constructing various shelters for her latest amateur farmer project. She didn't always meet with success, like the time she tried to build a small protection for her chickens. It proved no match for the raccoons or foxes that broke right though and ate up every chicken! Their house was their gym.

As for myself, as an extreme introvert, I'm not interested – at all – in going to a gym full of people. I did train outdoors for years with a great personal trainer (Ace Morgan, for those of you in the Bay Area). Even though it was beautiful to train in the park every week with Ace, and I love Ace – he is an amazing guy! – I still hated going, because, well, I hate "exercise!" I knew that I had to find something that I loved to do that happened to be exercise.

The only sport I could ever think of that came close was swimming. I love to swim! I did get to swim every day when I lived with my grandma for about a year in Los Alamitos. But in San Francisco, pools are few and far between, and definitely not the introvert-friendly private backyard pool like at Gramma's house!

Anyway, I FINALLY FOUND A THING THAT I REALLY ENJOY THAT IS EXERCISE! For me, salvation came in the form of a virtual reality headset! After reading an article online about some VR exercise apps, I decided to go for it. I got my own VR (the Oculus Quest 2, for which I wish I could monetize my referrals – I have recommended that thing to so many people).

There are some decent exercise apps for the Oculus, but there is only one that I keep returning to over and over, every single day. I still look forward to it and cheerfully follow the instructions of my virtual coaches! Since starting with the Oculus, I have also been monitoring my heart health on a smart watch. Well, the numbers don't lie. My heart has been getting healthier. My weight is slowly dropping (about a pound a week) and I am really surprised at how much it has helped my mental focus and attitude!

The app that I am enamored with is called Supernatural. It appeals to me as a world class introvert. The environments you're placed in are huge spacious landscapes, either real or fantasy locations. The exercise is set to the rhythm of decent music. The ever positive and encouraging coaches are great. The VR workout is perfect for my animal brain.

My neocortex knows that I am holding little plastic hand controllers that weigh about 9 ounces a piece. I am certain that I look utterly ridiculous in the real world, swatting my arms around to seemingly random beats. But within my limbic system, I am triumphantly standing alone in some incredible location. I powerfully slash through targets with my lethal sporty light bats. I am in perfect time with the beat of songs that seem way better in the virtual world than they do in a Lyft or in a retail store!

I find myself really believing in the coaches' positive affirmations. You can do it! Warrior!

And it really does help me to head into the day and push to achieve more! No lie, the fact that I am really writing this book is a testament to the power of getting more energy and focus through moving my body. It is incredible.

There are many ways to improve your posture and lots of professionals who can help you fine tune it even more! Alexander Technique is one of the best methods if you are looking specifically to improve your posture. Certain chiropractors specialize in postural improvement. There are plenty of gizmos, corsets, and electronic devices (like shock collars for people with bad posture) that you can use to train yourself.

But here are some really simple tips. If you are reading this book, it's likely that you are spending too much time in a forward flexed position. I can pretty much guarantee that you spend so much time with your head forward that you are losing the natural C-shaped curve in your cervical spine (your neck). This means that your neck extensors – the muscles that cause your neck to extend backwards - are weak and need more support.

Here is a simple isometric exercise that can help with this. Isometric exercises are those in which your muscles are engaged, but you don't appear to be moving anywhere. For this exercise, you will put one hand flat on the back of your head and then you will push your head backwards into your hand. Your head will not actually go anywhere, but you should feel the extensor muscles of your neck engage.

In the body, most skeletal muscles have an opposing muscle. The active muscle is called the agonist, and the opposing muscle is called the antagonist. When the agonist muscle activates, its antagonist naturally relaxes. Otherwise, you would have a hard time moving anywhere. So, when the extensor muscles activate, you can feel the flexors relax. As they relax, you might be surprised to feel the relief, since you may not have been aware that they were being overly stressed in the first place!

Do this isometric exercise for about 30 seconds or so several times a day, especially when you are spending a lot of time at a computer. If you find yourself sitting or standing against a wall, you can also just press your head straight backward into the wall. Warning: if you wear a lot of product in your hair, then beware the possibility of leaving an awkward head mark on the wall.

Another simple thing that you can do to help improve the curve in the neck is to just lay down (face up) on your bed and let your head hang off the edge. Don't do this if it gives you a headache or makes you dizzy, and don't do it for too long! Just a few minutes will give your neck some traction and extension. A more gentle method is to roll up a towel into a little log shape and put in under your neck while you're on your back. This gives some gentle traction and supports extension as well.

On the flip side, here are the worst things you can do for you neck. Number one: sleeping on your stomach! This. Is. The.

Worst. There is practically no point in even going to a chiropractor if you do this. Since you can't breathe with your face planted straight into your pillow, your neck is forced to turn way over to one side or the other while you are sleeping. This causes one side to be too loose and one side to be tight. You have permanent imbalance, and even if you do get adjusted, the adjustment does not hold very well.

After stomach sleeping, the next worst thing is couch sleeping! Why are you falling asleep on the couch? Don't do it. I know, but it's so comfortable. Couches are the worst. They are "comfortable," yet they screw up your body if you spend too much time on them, whether it's sitting or sleeping. Just don't do it.

Speaking of sleep, a lot of people ask me what the best mattress and pillows are! My answer is, "a good one." Sorry. People's bodies and preferences vary so much that I don't think there is a real specific answer! But as with food and everything else, use your common sense.

A really cheap mattress is a terrible idea. A really cheap pillow is a terrible idea. They're just going to degrade quickly and lose whatever little support they originally gave. That being said, the most expensive mattresses and pillows are not necessarily the best, either. Pick a decent one – best if you have a chance to try one out first – and one with a decent warranty or even an initial 30-90 day no questions asked return policy.

If a pillow or a mattress company offers to take it back no questions asked within 30-90 days of nightly use, then they are offering a decent product. Your mattress might be the most important piece of major furniture that you buy, so don't skimp!

The topic of "sleep" overlaps the good S.E.C.S. subcategories. We'll revisit the topic again, but I'm going to go ahead and mention that timing is an important part of healthy sleep. Most people set an alarm for when to wake up. This is ok, although you shouldn't really need to set an alarm if you're getting enough sleep.

But what would be even better is to set an alarm *for when to go to sleep!* Most people put off their bedtime until too late.

They also spend too much screen time too close to bedtime. The blue light from the screens can interfere with the circadian rhythm. A lot of phones now have a yellowish screen setting for "night mode." This is a good innovation, but you know what's better? No screen time at all before bed. So determine what time you want to get ready for bed. Set your alarm for the "screen off" time. When that alarm goes off, turn off your devices and do your bedtime routine. Maybe you take a shower, knock out a short meditation, read a good old-fashioned book.

What time should you set your sleep alarm? Ideally? Around 8pm. No kidding. The goal should be to be in bed and falling asleep between 9-11pm, but much closer to the 9pm side. In Chinese medicine, this is adrenal time on the 24-hour body clock. If you can be resting and asleep during this time, you will find that you get a lot more bang for your restfulness buck! I find that if I get to bed by 9, I can wake up around 4:30am feeling incredibly rested – like I've "slept in!"

I feel so much more restful than I do if I go to sleep closer to midnight and wake up around 7:30am. It's the same 7.5 hours of sleep, but it feels so different to the body!

Some of you may think that getting up at 4:30am sounds terrible, but it is amazing. Those early morning hours are easily the most productive hours of my day. They are so quiet. Nobody is calling or texting me, my kid is asleep, the world is quiet. This is the best time for focused personal work.

By the time 8 or 9am rolls around and the standard workday is beginning, you've already accomplished a lot. The main resistance I hear about getting to bed early is that late night is the only time when people feel like they can get that "me" time. Well, I'm here to tell you that if you flip that "me" time around onto the other side of the day, you will never regret it! Why give yourself the last dregs of the energy left over from the long day? Give yourself the best and the freshest energy of the day! Start with you!

As a chiropractor, you would think that I would want to keep all the secrets of structural self-care to myself, but I think that is crazy. There is a chiropractor in Michigan who has a great series of videos on YouTube. He shows you various ways to release your own spine. It's not quite self-adjusting, but it's the closest you can safely get. His name is Dr. Michael Rowe and his YouTube channel is called SpineCare Decompression and Chiropractic Center. I hope that it stays up for as long as this book exists. And oh well, if it doesn't, I'm sure that someone else has taken up the mantle. Unless it's the real apocalypse and someone is reading this stray book found in a dry desert cave somewhere. If so, well, sorry about that. You can still push your head into your hand. Shit, if it's the real apocalypse, then you probably don't have any problem whatsoever with your neck being too far in flexion. Well, good for you then, future post-apocalyptic reader!

The other big structural consideration is on the other side of your body. It's your feet and legs. Your feet and legs have a huge impact on your spine and your posture. Because we are spending way too much time sitting, the muscles on the backs of our legs, particularly the hamstrings, are too tight and short. This puts a lot of strain on the low back. People think they want some stretches for their low back, but really, they should be spending more time on stretching their legs, hips and feet!

Most people stretch their hamstrings by standing and touching (or attempting to touch) their toes. If you prefer a standing stretch, you can get a more dynamic stretch by bending your knees, resting your elbows on your thighs, and then slowly straightening your legs.

You can get an even better stretch by taking the weight off of your legs and stretching while laying down. Lay down on your back and use a towel, rope or exercise band wrapped around your foot to pull your leg backwards into a stretch. The reason that you can get a better hamstring stretch while you're laying down goes back to that concept of agonists and antagonists.

While you're standing, your hamstrings are somewhat engaged, because you are in the weightbearing position. They can't really relax all the way, and if you're wanting to stretch them, then you do want them to relax! If you're looking to work with a stretching specialist, I recommend working with an Active Isolated Stretching specialist. This is a fantastic approach that involves stretching a muscle while its opposite antagonist muscle is engaged.

My experience with this type of stretching is that after the work is done, I always feel like I've just had a great massage, but the effects last a lot longer! The lazy part of me just wants to lay down on a table and let someone else do all the work. But with Active Isolated Stretching, there is no passive laying around. You have to do some work, too – by engaging the muscles. First world problems, right?

OK, so, do you want to get really real about how you're doing with posture and how you are physically showing up in the world? The simplest, fastest and perhaps most painful way to find out is to video yourself standing, walking and speaking! Holy moly. You will likely discover some uncomfortable truths. Now, I'm not going to win any awards for poise and statuesqueness myself, but considering where I started, I feel pretty good about where I'm at!

I learned a lot about correcting my posture for success while I was *in* chiropractic school, but, not *from* chiropractic school. I mean, I learned the theories. But nothing kicked my ass into action like the horror of watching myself on video during acting classes at the Alliance Theatre School!

Acting was never an interest of mine. In fact, it terrified me. Yet I was always enrolled in a class at the Alliance Theatre School in Atlanta starting with my 2nd trimester of chiropractic school. I signed up as soon as I learned that part of chiropractic school involved public speaking. I was mortified. I couldn't even fathom it. So I wanted to learn and train as far away from the eyes of my peers as possible. In Atlanta, nobody would know me.

I ended up enjoying the classes. I made some new friends. I even developed a side-hustle. I had a short-lived career as a birthday party clown, costumed character and "promotional performer." This was all in my quest to be able to give a simple patient health lecture without passing out or bursting into tears!

Part of the film acting classes (as opposed to the stage acting classes) involved filming ourselves and watching the footage together. Ouch. What the hell was going on with my left arm there? What was I doing with my face? My slouch? My mumbly mouth and shifty eyes! Just shoot me already.

I learned to make the necessary adjustments, holding my arms in places that felt awkward to me at first, but which looked relaxed on camera. I learned to hold my body and my shoulders in positions that also felt awkward at first but that looked right on camera.

I had been conditioned to feel comfortable in that curled over introvert geek mode. I was biomechanically suited to writing letters to my many pen-pals and messaging my nerdy BBS friends. I needed to shift to be able to look good standing up and interacting face-to-face with other people in "the real world." (Although if it exists, it's all real, right?)

I learned to use my voice in a way that sounded too loud and bold to my usual self, but which sounded correct on camera. I learned that as I changed my body and how I presented physically in the world, the world responded differently to me!

This upset my punk rock ethos, and I had an impulse to rebel against it. Screw you conformists! Sheeple! Zombies! You're so fake! But no, not fake or sheeple or whatever – just humans. Remember, we're animals, too. We respond unconsciously to cues that we've learned over countless generations! There's no shame in being animals, because that's what we are. And there's also no shame in learning how it works and working it.

The genie is already out of the bottle.

Yes, we have magical superpowers (sort of) and it is just up to us whether we want to use our powers for good or for evil. I say let's use them for good. Shit will still happen, so, why not at least make a good go of it for the light?

So, shoot yourself on video. If you look and feel great, well, good for you. If you don't feel so good, don't worry. There's always a solution! Just make the corrections as you see fit, re-shoot the video and repeat. You will get better and better on your own. But to really take it to the next level, consider working with a postural and movement specialist such as an Alexander Technique instructor to quickly master posture.

Of course, as a chiropractor, I am in favor of chiropractic adjustments as a part of structural health. I'm not sure what the controversy is considering that idea. It's weird to me that some people believe that the body *can't* subluxate, or misalign, while negatively affecting the function.

I had a patient who was having a lot of shoulder pain, which he first went to his primary physician for since it was so painful. In addition to the pain, he had lost some strength in the right shoulder. The physician didn't find anything wrong with it and suggested that the patient just take some ibuprofen. They took some x-rays, but nothing appeared to be out of the ordinary. When the patient came to my office, we quickly deduced that his shoulder was subluxated. The A/C (or acromioclavicular) joint had moved slightly forward from its proper position. Following a specific adjustment to the A/C joint, the patient's pain immediately reduced, and he had strength again in his right shoulder.

When he went back to his primary care physician to report that the shoulder had been subluxated, and that a chiropractic adjustment had corrected it, she told him that that was not possible.

"The shoulder can't subluxate," she said, "It can only dislocate."

Our bodies are not digital – all zeros and ones. We're analog. There are curvy lines and grey areas all around. There is a distance to be traveled between great alignment and dislocation! The grey area in between is the home of the subluxation, and that's a very real place.

Subtle structural imbalances over years and years create big problems. Imagine the simple case of needing a hip replacement. Both of those hips are the same age, but why did one of them wear out so much faster?

There are *many* different approaches to chiropractic and styles of chiropractic out there! I won't even try to get into what they are and how they work. But one thing I will say about chiropractic is that it is a testament to the power of how changing the structure can change almost anything.

One of my colleagues from chiropractic school, Dr. Judd Nogrady, co-wrote a book called *Cast to be Chiropractors*. In this book, he tells the story of how he was originally a New York City police officer with pretty serious anger issues. It was a single powerful chiropractic adjustment to his C1 vertebra that released something inside of him. His deep-seated anger, which he had struggled with for so long, just dissipated. It was such a profound healing experience for him that he made the dramatic profession swap from cop to chiropractor!

As for myself, I have seen it in my own office and experienced it in my own body. When the structure of the body is in good working condition, life is better all around.

Emotions

The second letter of our good S.E.C.S. model is, in my opinion, the most important of them all!

It is the biggie.

If you are healthy emotionally, then the body can override a multitude of sins. I can't even tell you how many times this happens.

Some people have to keep incredibly strict diets due to health issues. Then they travel to places where they are in a different emotional state. Suddenly, their body treats food differently. They are able to eat foods comfortably which otherwise would give them trouble! But then when they are back home, the old problems revert.

I see this all the time with people who have wheat and dairy sensitivity issues. They struggle with wheat and dairy sensitivity on a daily basis. But then they go on vacation to France and suddenly everything changes. They find that even though they are eating wheat and dairy their digestion seems to be fine!

What is that about?

At first, I thought that it was because European wheat and dairy must be cleaner or genetically superior to what we have here. This is possible, as Europe generally does not use genetically modified crops. But could there be an emotional component as well? How is your emotional state different if you're on a European vacation? How is the general emotional state around food different in France compared to that in the US?

Digestion is just one of the systems affected by changes in emotional state. Other things that can shift are body pains, muscle spasms, allergies – almost any symptom you can think of.

I had a patient once who had chronic neck pain which we were certain stemmed from an old motorcycle injury. But a strange thing happened. Whenever he left San Francisco, the neck pain went away! I mean, it was like leaving a magical boundary. As he crossed one of the bridges out of the city, his neck pain would fade, and once he was out, it was gone!

Clearly, there must have been an emotional connection.

In cases like this, the solution is usually to use a method called Neuro Emotional Technique (NET). NET is a stress-reducing technique developed by Dr. Scott Walker. NET uses biofeedback in the form of manual muscle testing to discover the hidden causes of emotional stress responses in the body. Then it uses a simple CTRL-ALT-DEL type of approach to desensitize the stress response.

If you want to see a great example of NET in action, see if you can watch Grey's Anatomy, season 15 episode 22, "Head Over High Heels." When I heard that the episode would show one of the characters receiving an NET treatment, I cringed inside. I fully expected a sensationalized Hollywood approach to ensue! But to my great surprise and relief, they did a fantastic job with an eye for detail.

There is an increasing body of quality research to support NET. This includes a peer-reviewed fMRI study published in the Journal of Cancer Survivorship. And yet, NET still seems like magic. As a type 5 on the Enneagram (i.e. someone who has basically no idea what they are feeling emotionally in the moment), NET has been a godsend.

Traditional talk therapy, which works great for many people, does not work well for me because (1) I don't like to talk and (2) I don't know what I'm feeling. I sit uncomfortably in the chair, and I think hard about what I'm supposed to say. I keep looking at the clock, and sometimes ask if we can just call it a day at the 45-minute mark.

With NET, I can get a better sense of what I'm feeling thanks to the biofeedback of the manual muscle test. By seeing and feeling how my body responds to concepts of stress, I am better able to get in touch with those feelings and then to process them in a healthy way.

While the research supports it, you don't really need research to know that your emotional state has a big impact on the state of your health. And if it affects your health, then it affects your business.

When you're feeling positive and balanced emotionally, life seems to roll along more smoothly. You magically attract more business. The good kind of business! When you're in an emotionally terrible place, business often takes a bad turn as well. People who didn't even have appointments are calling in to cancel! You may develop a cold sore or new aches and pains.

Think about the people who you enjoy doing business with. Who do you like to refer business to? When you think about people who seem to be in an emotionally bad space, do you want to send them business? Chances are, no. You don't trust that they will do a good job for your referrals. You don't want to get involved with the drama! If someone seems to be in a healthy emotional state, then you feel confident in sending them business. You feel good about it.

Emotional self-care involves proactive positive steps such as reading books or listening to podcasts about emotional health, practicing mindfulness and periodic check-ins with a professional.

It's impossible to get an objective look at yourself. You don't necessarily have to go to weekly therapy, although that is a part of many people's regular self-care. But it's good to see a mental health care professional once in a while. This is the same as seeing a physician once in a while to check in with your physical health.

Self-care techniques are important, too. These include meditation, mindfulness and making sure to have positive and supportive people in your life. It's also important to reduce or get rid of toxic relationships and conditions from your life. There are some emotionally toxic people that are hard to cut out, such as family members or people you are forced to work closely with. The good news is that getting your own head space cleared up does wonders for handling "difficult" people!

Here is a simple mindfulness exercise that I learned from Dr. Nick Campos. It is very powerful for helping to reduce the intensity of a stressful emotion.

Take a sheet of paper or open a blank document file. At the top of the page, write down the problem or the thing that is stressing you out. For example, "I am going bald." (This problem did cause me quite a lot of distress during the early days!) Next, make 4 columns. The first column is labeled "The worst thing about this problem." The second column is labeled "The best thing about this problem." The third column is labeled, "The worst thing about if this problem did not exist." And the fourth column is labeled, "The best thing about if this problem did not exist."

Next, write 20 things under each column! If 20 is too hard, then write 10. But you will get a lot more out of the exercise if you can find 20! It's OK if they're ridiculous, as long as they're true for you. For me and the going bald issue, the first lines might read something like this.

Worst thing: It accentuates my small potato shaped head. Best thing: I will save a lot of money on shampoo. Worst thing if it never happened: I might have been a vain douche canoe with no compassion for bald guys. Best thing if it had never happened: I would have continued to enjoy my cute hair.

Worst thing: I will have an even harder time attracting a cute partner. Best thing: I will not have to go to a hairdresser anymore. Worst thing if it never happened: I would have had to see a hairdresser forever. Best thing if it had never happened: I would have continued to network regularly with hairdressers.

It's crazy how writing things out like that reveals inner conflicts that you were oblivious to. I had no idea that I had so many mixed feelings about hairdressers! The main purpose of the exercise, though, is really to have a neutralizing effect on the thing that is stressing you out. Once you have so many pros and cons listed out, whatever it is seems a lot less extreme, and therefore less stressful.

Here is another great stress-reducing technique developed through the Neuro Emotional Technique world. It's called the First Aid Stress Tool, or, FAST. Go to www.firstaidstresstool.com to see a video on how it's done.

In a nutshell, here is the procedure. First, identify an issue that is stressing you out. For example, the big jump in health insurance premiums for your staff! It may be helpful to ask yourself how intense the stressful feeling is, on a scale of one to ten? Is it a seven? A ten? Next, put one of your wrists (palm up) into your other hand. Using three fingers of your bottom hand, gently wrap your fingers around your wrist as if to take a pulse. (You probably will feel a pulse, too.) Next, put the open palm against your forehead, centering it between the eyebrows and the hairline. Now, take a few deep breaths while focusing on the *feeling* of the stressful thing. After a few good deep breaths, switch hands and repeat. Check in again with the intensity of the stress. Where is it now on that one to ten scale? Did it drop down a notch? More than likely, it probably dropped down several notches!

Recently, I saw a patient who was recovering from a heart attack. He was unable to drive himself to the appointment, so he came along with a friend. The friend was living in one of the tent communities nearby. He didn't have any steady income, so he was working as a caregiver for my patient.

While waiting for the patient to finish his appointment, the friend squirmed in his chair. He couldn't get comfortable. He, too, had chronic back pain. He asked if I took Medi-Cal. He wasn't looking for a handout but was hoping for some relief. I said that I did, but that unfortunately they only allow two visits a month. I wasn't sure that we could make much headway on a longstanding problem in two visits a month.

In my head, I was also thinking, I also don't know how much we can do with the ongoing stress of living in a tent encampment! As luck would have it, though, the exam revealed that his back pain was indeed stress related. We were able to get a lot of relief in that one visit. He was blown away.

I showed him how to do FAST. I told him that any time he felt the stress rising, he should do it, and that it would help his body to process the stress. Two weeks later, he returned, again accompanying his friend. His back was still doing well, and he excitedly thanked me for showing him how to do FAST.

"Last week, someone pissed me off real bad, and I was so mad I thought I was going to lose my mind! I just wanted to break something! I was so mad. But then I remembered that thing you taught me, and I did it, and then all of a sudden, I wasn't mad anymore! I felt good! This shit works! This shit really works! Thank you so much!"

He later had a falling out with his friend, and I never saw him again. But I hope that he taught other people how to do FAST! In my perfect world fantasy, things like FAST are taught in kindergarten. Something so simple that can help so much should be universal knowledge!

A lot of people do FAST right before bed each night, and report that it helps tremendously with processing the stress of the day. I had a young patient, about 7 years old, who was having a lot of nightmares and started using FAST before bed. I asked her if it seemed to be helping with her stress, and she said, "I don't know...' but then she added, "The main thing it does is it makes me have no more nightmares." No more nightmares! I would say that's a win.

I have had many clients over the years who have eliminated some very extreme nightmares – night terrors – through using NET. One of the patients had such extreme night terrors that she would scream in her sleep. It caused everyone else in the household to wake up and run and see if she was OK! But she would always fall back asleep and then have no memory of the screaming in the morning. This poor woman was not even aware of her own screaming and nightmare activity at night, but her family was at their wits end! Even though she didn't remember the nightmares, her body certainly did, so using NET, we were able to find the root and stop the nightmares. The root cause was a series of highly traumatic wartime incidents that her brain was reliving over and over, every night.

Emotional health, by the way, is not only about feeling good. All the emotions – even the "bad" ones like anger and fear – are actually neutral. They are neither good nor bad – they just are. There are times and places where anger and fear are totally appropriate and therefore good. Occasionally, someone will come in and want to do NET to make a negative feeling "go away" such as grief following the loss of a loved one. But sometimes the muscle test doesn't show that anything needs to be "cleared" at all. Not all bad feelings are NECs (Neuro Emotional Complexes). Sometimes, it's just the right feeling to be having at the that time.

Journaling is another great tool for processing emotions. There are no rules on what or how to write. It's just for you. Some people write down their thoughts or their feelings. Some people write poetry. Some people draw simple doodles. The idea is to get stuff that's inside of your head out so that you can look at it from another angle.

Chemistry

Each of the categories that makes up the good S.E.C.S. can easily fill a book on its own! I feel like I keep saying that. But it's true. The chemistry category includes food, nutrition, toxicity, hormones, brain chemistry. All of it. It's incredibly complicated. But, in the words of Sweet Brown... ain't nobody got time for that!

In business, in life and even when it comes to your body chemistry, the Pareto principle applies. 80% of the consequences are coming from 20% of the causes. You don't have to be 100% perfect. You don't even need to hit 80%. If you hit the most consequential 20%, then you'll end up doing pretty well. The thing about this 20% though is that it's not so much about THE 20% as it is about YOUR 20%. The things that make the biggest impact are different for everyone. This is based on the unique hand of genetic cards that you were handed. Figuring it out is all part of the journey.

Your animal brain wants to know that food is abundant and readily available in your environment. That is one of **the** most basic needs. Ditto with water. Your animal brain feels good knowing that there is clean and abundant water where you live. It wants to know that it's safe to go to sleep where you live. That nothing will cut your throat while you slumber! And yes, it wants to get laid once in a while. If you're an extrovert, it wants a lot of friends or family all around. And if you're an introvert, it wants to know that there are friends out there, at a distance, but available.

But, you say, I do eat, I drink water, I sleep, but my reptile brain is an asshole – so is my mammal brain – and my body still feels like crap! What am I doing wrong? Remember, we're trying to speak the primitive language of the deep brain. It developed over hundreds of thousands of years! Let's be honest. A lot of what we're passing off as "food" these days is not, in fact, food.

What's everyone's favorite food? Pizza, amiright? Pizza seems like great food. The best food. But, unless you're eating some fancy artisanal good stuff, that flour is not really a thing that would register as real "food" to our ancestors. Read *Wheat Belly*, by William Davis. Even setting aside the refining process, which itself is problematic, the plant itself is practically an alien species. It's genetically alien from the wheat that our grandparents were eating when they were kids. Modern wheat is so unnatural that it can't even survive on its own in the wild. It's sterile and its seeds don't grow into new healthy wheat plants. So, there's that.

The biggest part of the pizza (unless you like those weird super deep pizzas that are like tomato sauce pies) is not ideal human food. What about the sauce? Doesn't that count as vegetables? Setting aside the fact that tomatoes are fruits, no, the sauce isn't that healthy, either. Again, unless you're eating some fancy artisanal stuff, there are so many additives. A few of the most common are sugar, colors and preservatives.

And do we even need to get into the sausage conversation? You know it can't be good. Why else would there be that saying, "I know how the sausage is made!" It's not good. Pizza is also very dehydrating, as far as foods go. The high sodium content and the dry crust work to pull hydration from our bodies.

So, even though it tickles all the primitive receptors in the mouth – mmm, salt, mmmmm, fat, mmmm, sweet.... nom nom nom – once it hits the gut, the body is like, "WTF, yo???" On that level, it most certainly does *not* tickle all the happy buttons. It leads to bad things. Inflammation, leaky gut, dehydration, gas, bloating, maybe constipation, maybe the trots. The body is kind of angry. Kind of at war with itself. It's unhappy and unhealthy, but damn that shit tastes good!

(I'm not hating on pizza, by the way. I love it as much as anyone. Just saying... the prevalence of foods like this in our diets mean there is a lot of room for improvement when it comes to our biochemistry!)

So while the gut is dealing with food on mechanical and chemical levels, the mammalian brain is lost in the world of *feelings* about the food. This brain remembers smells and tastes and sounds and puts it all together in the world of feelings. The sense of smell is the most powerful of all. A familiar scent can instantly bring up memories of a time or place long forgotten. The smell of birthday cake. Parties. Good times, celebrations. So, cake equals good. It may not make "the body" feel good in those other functional ways, but that's some other brain's job, isn't it?

The mammal brain is all in the feels. It goes with familiarity. Foods that went with stable and relatively safe places are good things. Foods that seem alien or that went with places that were "other" might not be so appealing. If a food goes with a feeling, then the animal brain will tend to go with that food. If there's no feeling, just the neocortex saying, "We really should choose the dark leafy green thing" then the animal brain wins. Food is such a powerful driver that instinct and habit will win over logic every time.

To make matters worse, there is a "second brain" in the gut. A big part of how the gut brain functions is directly related to the gut biome. The gut biome is the ecosystem of all the various living critters down there! Yes, we are like our own bizarre little planet! There are villages and maybe even countries down there. Certain kingdoms and tribes are peaceful, and some of them are just assholes. Even though you're better off with the peaceful kingdoms, if the asshole kingdoms dominate, then guess what? You're going to feel very strangely compelled to move towards the sorts of foods and beverages that support the life of the assholes!

This is also why when you try to do a cleanse and come off of those "bad" foods, etc., the body can actually feel *worse* at first. You can experience worse headaches, body pain, anxiety, moodiness. Why? Because as the asshole kingdoms inside of you are dying, they are basically screaming and launching their little bioterror weapons and making you suffer! They're making demands to let them live and take over again! Circle of life man, it's brutal.

Before we get into "what" to eat, we need to get really clear on one thing.

We're not logical.

None of us. Zero. Not me, not you. It's not personal. Accept it. There's no point in getting upset about it. See, if you get upset about it, you're proving the point. Just take a deep breath. It's ok. Once you can accept – really accept! – that you're not nearly as rational as you think you are, then the food thing becomes less of a struggle. (To learn more about how your brain is really anything but logical, I recommend the book *Idiot Brain: What Your Head Is Really up To*, by Dean Burnett.)

When we're immersed in an environment, it's easy to simply accept it as "normal." This is one of the reasons why traveling to foreign countries is so great. It's very eye-opening! A couple of years ago, I discovered that hosting foreign guests for a few days can be almost the same as visiting another country.

In 2018, a Russian couple who I had befriended through Postcrossing stayed with me for a couple of days during their whirlwind visit to the US. I may be a world-class introvert, but I also pride myself on being an excellent host – up to a maximum of 72 hours. I took them all over the city and across the bay to see Muir Woods. I wanted to make sure that whenever we stopped for food, it would be good stuff!

I noticed that Timofey and Violetta would only ever order a warm tea and then basically split an appetizer. Sometimes they would get soup. At first, I thought that they were being thrifty travelers. I marveled at their tiny "luggage." They basically had two small duffle bags for their entire trip! They looked more like they were headed to the gym than to a two-week international vacation! If it were me traveling, my CPAP machine and books alone would have taken up more space!

By the second day, I finally brought up the subject of the food. I told them that I would be happy to pay for their meal, and that they could order whatever they wanted. I told them that I noticed that they only ordered appetizers or soup to share. I wondered if they were trying to save money.

They laughed at me and said, no! They couldn't understand how Americans could eat so much food! They said that American portions are too big, and that they wouldn't feel good if they tried to eat that much food at one meal!

When I tried to imagine shrinking my portions down to the size of what my Russian friends were living on, my brain resisted mightily. I felt internal pushback. Anger. Anxiety. I could tell that these feelings were irrational. But it didn't make them any less real.

After Timofey and Violetta went back to Yekaterinburg, I decided to try out "the Russian diet" for a month. My "Russian diet" was just to cut my portion size in half of what I would have ordinarily eaten.

The results? I felt fine!

Physically, I felt good. I felt lighter and more clear-headed. I saved a lot of money! My food expenditures were almost cut in half. I say "almost" because I was still paying for my son's food for about half the week. The only real resistance came from my mind. My mind would panic a little when it saw that I wasn't going to eat the full meal. There was an internal discomfort that I realized was purely mental and emotional. When I checked in with my physical body, there was nothing wrong. It felt fine with the amount of food that I was eating. If I was hungry later, then I would eat.

But as I moved away from the autopilot mode of eating what I had been accustomed to eating, my mind felt very uncomfortable. It doesn't like changes tied to survival. I thought that I would maintain my "Russian diet" indefinitely, but of course I slid back into the "American diet" after a few meals with friends and an unconscious return to normal.

The animal brain does what the animal brain does. There's no point in beating yourself up for it. Your cat certainly doesn't lose any sleep over it if you get upset that it's not sticking to a new system that you've set up! The cat is just a cat. Your animal brain is like that, too. So slow down, keep breathing, and keep on keeping on.

If food habits are your struggle, then I recommend Eliza Kingsford's book, *Brain-Powered Weight Loss: The 11-Step Behavior-Based Plan That Ends Overeating and Leads to Dropping Unwanted Pounds for Good*. While the title is aimed at people who are looking to lose weight, the book is a great read for anyone who's ever had a hard time with food or with proper care and feeding of the human animal. She draws from years of clinical experience, the latest findings in neurology and manages to be informative and scientific without putting you to sleep! Highly recommended.

For as long as human eyeballs are reading this book, I guarantee 100% that the basics of human nutrition remain the same. We mostly know the basics, though we like to act like we don't! Really? A baked sweet potato with a little sea salt and butter is healthier than deep-fried sweet potatoes smothered in marshmallow sauce? Is that so, now? Really? A freshly grilled fish caught locally today is healthier than a microwaved frozen platter of breaded tilapia that was caught in Thailand weeks ago? Come on. We know this.

But one thing that most of us do not know is that it matters – a lot! – *how* we are eating and *who we are being* while we are eating. Some of the basics of how we are eating make sense, and some of them don't. But bear with me. If you do it, you'll feel the difference.

Marc David, in his book *Mind/Body Nutrition*, is all about *how* we eat and who we are being while we eat. I highly recommend it. Most of us tend to eat very quickly and miserably. We are stressed when we eat. But think about it. As animals, what happens when we're stressed? The body goes into fight-flight mode. The digestive system slows down. Energy is diverted to the muscles so that you can run or fight! Now is not the time to be leisurely digesting a meal!

So, if you want to digest a meal, then you have to let your body know that you're not fighting anything. It's all good. Since the body doesn't understand language, you have to speak to it in a language that it does understand. It understands signals such as breathing. So when you're about to eat, sit down – don't stand – and take a few deep breaths.

Marc David recommends taking ten slow deep breaths before every meal. When I read this, it didn't sound too bad. But when I first tried it, I felt like that cartoon owl from the 1970s Tootsie Pop commercial. He tries to count the licks it takes to get to the center of a Tootsie Pop! One... two... [chomp!] three. It takes three licks.

After about three deep breaths, I caught myself getting incredibly impatient and thinking, "WHO HAS TIME FOR 10 BREATHS BEFORE EVERY MEAL????" When I say it out loud, it sounds ridiculous. But that's how it feels! The body strongly resists any and all deviations from its normal! It's soooo uncomfortable.

What is the problem? What are we waiting for? Why are you being slow?

We've been conditioned to be in a state of fight or flight. Well, the only path to change is... to change! So you just have to do it. You will feel the calm and the change.

The experience of eating the meal will indeed be different. Maybe this is why saying grace before meals became a thing and remains an important part of mealtime for many people. Yes, it's always great and healthy to adopt the attitude of gratitude! But it's also a way of putting in that quiet time and focus before a meal, to let the body know that all is well, and that it's safe to eat.

Besides deep breathing before a meal, it makes a big difference if you can make sure that you are always eating in a nice environment. Not everyone has the luxury, but I know that whatever you are doing, you can do better. If you're eating at your work desk, quit it. Just don't. It's not beautiful, and it doesn't make your brain or body feel any better about it.

It can be a little folding tray table with a little tablecloth and a flower in a vase. Even a fake flower, if you have a black thumb like me. It gives your brain – and therefore your body – the feeling of being somewhere different and special. It gives the feeling that this meal is special. The body will know that it is safe to digest it and assimilate the good that it has to offer. Turn off your phone or put it in airplane mode while you're eating. Unless you are waiting for some truly life and death information, the world can wait for you to finish your meal. After all, if you were just stuck in a tunnel on a stalled train for 20 minutes, you would have been equally unreachable. Then what would they have done? They would have had to wait and get over it. You don't have to be available 24/7 unless you're working a 24-hour type of shift as a firefighter or an emergency responder!

Another important aspect of mindful eating is to really enjoy what you're eating. Eat what you're going to eat, but make it the best, and savor it!

One of the basics for healthy body chemistry is (don't shoot the messenger) that most people need to reduce their caffeine intake. In most cases, this means cutting down on the coffee. Heresy! I know, I know! Sorry.

If you don't looove the coffee, then you've got to find another way to get your energy up. If you do loooove the coffee, then find a way to keep loving it, but while treating your body well and giving your body a better experience of it at the same time.

For example, a lot of people "love coffee" but buy cheap coffee so that they can drink a larger volume and get the desired caffeine kick from it. Some people even water down their coffee so that it will last longer throughout the day! When asked if they enjoy drinking this water coffee, the answer is usually "not really." Who likes coffee water?! So if you love coffee, then buy the BEST coffee beans – the ones that give you a little coffeegasm when you open the bag and smell the aroma. And make the BEST damn tiny cup of coffee. Savor the heck out of it. Make it something that you genuinely get serious joy from, that makes you feel like you are living the life. Knowing that this coffee you are drinking is as good as any coffee that anyone in the world could be drinking! The Queen of England herself could not be drinking a better cup of coffee. (Is she even a coffee drinker, or does she stick to tea? I don't know.)

If you're just craving something for that energy boost, well, find something else. I recommend a good adrenal supplement, such as Awakening formula, by Oxygen Nutrition. It does contain caffeine, but it won't give the same coffee highs and lows. It also contains adaptogens and herbs which help to support the adrenal glands.

Eat as many wild foods as possible. I am a big fan of wild foods! Wild foods are incredible. (Play Duran Duran's Wild Boys while you're eating them. It will make you feel like you're in an 80's adventure movie.) Wild foods are the sorts of food that our ancestors were eating long before we figured out how to cultivate it ourselves. Check out Jo Robinson's great book, *Eating on the Wild Side: The Missing Link to Optimum Health,* for a great intro to eating foods that are as close as possible to their wild originals.

Wild foods are usually incredibly healthy, packed with antioxidants and nutrients. They are tough and hardy because they have to be to survive in the wild! They survive without any cultivation at all. They are perfectly adapted to wherever they are growing. They fend off pests and disease without any help whatsoever from humans. They are far more abundant than you think.

It's mind blowing how many plants that we thought were just weeds are actually healthy foods. They are healthier than that the spicy pricey salad mix down at Whole Paycheck! Then why haven't we heard of these superfoods?

There are many reasons why these healthy wild foods are not found on our grocery shelves. For one thing, that's why – the shelf problem. These wild foods often have a very short shelf life, and they do not travel well. Once they're harvested, they need to be prepared and eaten fairly quickly. Also, a lot of them have a bitter taste that we do not get real excited about.

Culturally, we are all about the sweet and the salty in America. In some cultures, they have a deeper appreciation of sour and bitter. Not so much here. And yet, bitter is one of the highly therapeutic tastes that we are missing and that could make us a whole lot healthier! And finally, yard weeds are just not that sexy. It's hard to market a thing that is associated with boring weeds. What's the point of marketing something that almost everyone can find for free by just walking around their yard, neighborhood or local park?

I'm lucky to have a fantastic reference guide to foraging here in the San Francisco Bay Area. It's called *The Bay Area Forager: Your Guide to Edible Wild Plants of the San Francisco Bay Area* by Mia Andler and Kevin Feinstein. It is the ultimate guide to foraging in the Bay Area. I have taken a couple of

Kevin's classes with ForageSF (www.foragesf.com), and he is an incredible wealth of knowledge.

It's hard to explain the difference between eating food from the store versus wild food fresh from the dirt. There is a palpable sense of energy that is just so different from the experience of eating even the "best" produce from the store. It connects with something old and primal deep in the body. My brain still sometimes resists when I am in the backyard picking plantain weed, or cleavers for my smoothies.

But once I consume the thing, my body feels so good. I can feel a slight elevation in my mood, a slight drop in my inflammation, and I just feel good. I always think, that is so weird.

Plantain weed, by the way, is thus far my #1 favorite backyard superfood! If you have a yard, chances are, you have plantain weed somewhere in there. It grows all over the country. I remember it from when I lived in Virginia, and I have a distinct memory of digging it up as a kid and harvesting the leaves to eat. My mom denies this and says it never happened and that we didn't eat it. But I'm sticking to my story, especially after learning as an adult that not only is it edible but that it's ridiculously healthy!

Native people in California called it "panacea weed" because it was so good for so many things. One of its magic powers is that it works wonders on bug bites and stings. If you get a bug bite or sting, you just chew up some plantain weed leaf and make a spit poultice, spitting out the wad of chewed up leaf and put it on the itchy spot. You can cover it with a bandage and just leave it for a bit. I finally got to try this out one day when I got some kind of a little sting on my toe while out in the garden wearing sandals. I chewed up some plantain leaf and spit out the wad and put it on my toe, wondering how soon – if ever – the magic would kick in. I was impressed to discover that it kicked in almost immediately! I was blown away. The chewed-up plantain weed worked just as well – maybe even better – than store-bought anti-itch cream!

So why don't we use it? Again, shelf life and marketability. Would YOU rather buy chewed up plantain leaf to put on itches, or a nice cream that you don't see and that just washes away or fades over time? I also love frying the seed stalks of the plantain weed in butter and eating them as a snack. They have a nice flavor, like asparagus... which, I hear, is apparently what those big fat 18-year cicadas taste like, too. Don't worry. I won't get into foraging for bugs to eat here. Even I have some limits!

And here's another tip that is very important, regardless of what you are eating. It is this: CHEW YOUR FOOD! I mean, like, really chew it. Chewing is so significant that there was even a whole health craze about it back in the early 20th century, led by Horace Fletcher. Fletcher's motto was, "Nature will castigate those who don't masticate." His system of chewing was extreme, yet simple. There were only three rules:

1. Eat only when you have a good appetite.

2. Chew the food like pulp and drink that pulp. Do not swallow food.

3. Drink all liquids and liquid food sip by sip. Do not drink in gulps.

This method of chewing food into liquid pulp was called Fletcherizing. It takes forever, and the same impatient feeling creeps in as with the 10 deep breaths before the meal. Don't worry – you don't have to chew your food into liquid to feel better! You just have to do better than what you're doing right now.

When I first tried counting my chews, I was shocked to discover that left to my own devices, I was chewing my food an average of only two or three chomps before swallowing! Some say that Fletcher recommended a minimum of 25 chews per bite. Some say he recommended 100! Once you try 25, you see the 100 is probably the stuff of urban legend. But I saw that if I could shift my habit to somewhere between 3 and 25 chomps per bite, then I would be on my way.

Just chew your food thoroughly, and your digestion will improve. You will stop eating sooner than usual, too, because your brain's satiety center will have time to process the fact that you are full! You will also need fewer digestive enzymes and other supplements, as you start ingesting food in a more easily digestible form. You will also give your own enzymes, particularly the ones generated in the mouth, more time to be released and to do their job.

Diet fads come and go – always have, always will. Take them each with a grain of salt – preferably the nice raw sea variety. (My personal favorite is the Celtic Sea Salt.) But look for the timeless basics in the diets that are genuinely working for people.

Oh, this diet works, but you have to drink a lot of water and exercise? Oh, right. Pretty much no diets are successful without those "extras" such as water, exercise and sleep. This diet eliminates or cuts way down on refined carbs and grains. Right. How crazy, that foods which were artificially designed for shelf stability and pleasure sensor manipulation are not, in fact, nourishing and healthy foods! Mind. Blown. While I do, in fact, have a degree in nutrition, you do not need one to know where your diet can be improved.

Hydration is another one of those biggies in the body chemistry department! I think that we all know, generally speaking, about how much water we should be getting per day. "8 glasses a day" is what most people will tell you, and for a lot of people, this is about right.

(Although, for my dad, it was very wrong. I once asked him how much water he drank per day, and he said, "8 cups." I was surprised and impressed! And also skeptical, because he did not look like a man who drank 8 cups of water a day. So I asked him to show me these cups. Turns out, they were little bathroom Dixie paper cups! Barely bigger than a shot glass. My dad, a sweet guy with more than a touch of Asperger's, did not know what the problem was. Le sigh.)

Your recommended water intake is basically based on your body weight. There are two simple ways of calculating it that come out to roughly the same volume. The first is to take your weight (in pounds) and then divide that number by two. That is how many ounces of water per day that you should be aiming for. 8 cups a day (not Dixie cups) = 64 ounces/day = roughly 2 quarts. This is about what you need if you weigh about 130 pounds. If you weigh closer to the 180 mark, then it's more like 3 quarts. Average sized adults need between 2-3 quarts of water/day to feel good. The other way of calculating it is to say you need about 1 quart or about 1 liter per 50 pounds of body weight per day. If you are sweating a lot or it's hot outside, then you will likely need even more.

Even though I know this about water, I, too, sometimes slip in and out of good healthy water habits. Why? Because I'm human. When I'm on the water wagon, I find that my thinking is clearer. My muscles feel better – not as achy or tight. My skin feels and looks better. I don't get headaches. I don't crave as much sugar, and I am a generally more agreeable person. Yes, it's annoying to have to get up and pee when you'd rather be... what, sitting at your desk longer without a break?

Speaking of the peeing thing. You should not feel like you are just constantly peeing when you increase your water intake. It may happen in the beginning because you're not used to it. In essence, your body is like a dry sponge that doesn't immediately expand when you first pour water onto it.

If you're not getting enough water, your body thinks that there's a drought where you live, and it goes into water-conservation mode. It's not doing as many of the non-essential water-intensive activities. Things such as carrying away the metabolic waste materials from your muscles. So just because there's suddenly some more water available doesn't mean that your body instantly clicks into water utilization mode! You have to give it some time to trust that it's OK to use more water, seeing as it's apparently plentiful in your environment.

I can usually tell if a patient is dehydrated just by touching their spines. Dehydration creates a signature ropiness of the muscles. They're not smooth. They kind of feel like they're on their way to becoming beef jerky! Adjustments don't go as well, either, when the tissues are dehydrated. There's a rubbery feel to the joint play, and you often don't get that satisfying juicy ker-chunk of a great adjustment.

Speaking of drought conditions, you may sometimes wonder, how do people stay healthy who live in deserts and other arid places for years and years? The book *Quench: Beat Fatigue, Drop Weight, and Heal Your Body Through the New Science of Optimum Hydration* by Dana Cohen and Gina Bria explores this very topic. They reveal some surprising new information about hydration and how getting and staying hydrated is about more than just simple water intake!

They discuss how certain foods and smoothies work to maximize hydration while others deplete hydration. Perhaps one of the biggest revelations about hydration is the discovery of how water is delivered to the tissues of the body via the fascia. This means that exercise is an important part of staying hydrated, even though you lose some water by sweating!

Anyway, if you're drinking lots and lots of water but you are still just peeing it right out, there are a few other things that might be going on. Your electrolytes may be off, which is yet another of the many effects of stress. Part of the what the adrenal glands help to regulate is electrolyte balance. If your adrenals are shot due to chronic stress, then you will have a hard time with your electrolyte balance.

You can drink some electrolyte drinks (preferably without the sugar), or you can make your own using some of that nice Celtic sea salt I mentioned plus a little lemon juice. You can also just take a few pinches of the raw salt when you drink your water, and that will help. Raw unrefined salt with water after a workout is a great way to replenish electrolytes lost through sweating. It also helps to prevent sore muscles!

Some people use an even simpler rule of thumb for hydration. Pay attention to the color of your urine. If you are well hydrated, it will be very pale. If it's a bold yellow or a dark color, then you are not getting enough water. The darker the urine, the worse the condition. (If it's brown, you definitely need to get that checked out immediately!) If it's pink or reddish, hopefully you just ate some beets.

Do you need to drink special water? Alkaline water? Distilled? No – distilled water is a bad idea for drinking! This is because it's a little too pure, and thus it can tend to pull minerals out of your body. In chiropractic school, once in a while someone would hurt themselves from drinking too much distilled water. One girl passed out from the mineral depletion!

I do believe that most of us are running too acidic and need to push our body chemistry closer to alkaline. I also believe that many, if not most of the "hyper alkaline" waters out there right now are complete garbage. For a while, I was pretty into the BLK black alkaline water. Black water! How could an old goth like me resist? But one day, I decided to finally check the actual pH of the water.

Turns out, it was not super alkaline at all! It was barely more alkaline that my own tap water. I was ready to call the company and give them a piece of my mind! (Who am I kidding. I was going to e-mail them and give them a piece of my mind.) But then, I read the tiny print on the bottle. 9.5 pH measured at source. This means that they are only claiming that the alkaline pH was so at the source of the stream – not necessarily in the water that you were about to consume! So, I haven't bought any of the BLK water in a while. I was so irritated with the whole "measured at source" thing. But I still sigh wistfully when I pass it in the store. We could have been lovers. Forever! If only you didn't lie to me about your pH! So sad.

You can get as complicated or as simple as you like with the topic of water, so I'm going to leave it at that. Keep it simple, and your life and your business will be better.

Years ago, I used to speak every semester at City College to the Psych 101 class about mindbody medicine. In the nutrition section of my talk, I outlined a very simple program. At the end of my talk, I always gave the students the opportunity to come to the office for a free consultation.

Most of the students who chose to take me up on the offer opted to come in pretty soon. But one student made her appointment for about a month out, due to other commitments. When she finally came into the office, she came in beaming. She said that she hoped it was OK that she still came in even though she did not need the appointment anymore. She just wanted to come in and to thank me in person for doing that talk! Unlike every other student in attendance that day, she actually took the action steps.

She did ALL the things that I had talked about in my talk! She increased her water intake to the recommended levels. She eliminated sugar and alcohol from her diet. She reduced her grain and dairy intake. She increased her vegetables and fresh fruit intake. She went to sleep earlier.

When she had signed up for the free consultation, she had been suffering from a litany of problems. Joint pain, digestive issues, muscle spasms, anxiety, and insomnia. But over the course of about three weeks of following the new guidelines, she no longer had pain or anxiety. She was sleeping well. She was shocked and delighted to see that the whole time, the power to heal had been within herself already! She was better able to focus in school, too. Did changing her body change the course of her education and probably her future as a professional? Absolutely!

The basics are basic: eat simple meals with lots of vegetables – more vegetables than fruits – make it a 2 to 1 vegetable to fruit ratio. Vegetables are the least sexy food ever (well, you know, except I guess eggplants and cucumbers and such). But they are packed with powerful antioxidants, vitamins and minerals that keep your body and brain sharp and healthy! They also have fiber which keeps your pooper in good working order! You should eat foods in a state as close as possible to that in which they were harvested.

We touched on sleep earlier but sleep also deserves mention in the chemistry section. Good sleep is restorative to healthy chemistry. That's the way it's supposed to work. Bad sleep can both harm your chemistry (as in the case of sleep apnea, where you're not getting enough oxygen) and it can also be a sign of bad chemistry.

Blood sugar problems or liver stress can make you wake up suddenly in the middle of the night, usually between 1-3am. If you wake up every night in this time window, then take a look at your eating and drinking habits in the evening. Are you drinking wine at night? Try avoiding the wine or big dessert and see if you can sleep through that 1-3 time window. If the evening wine is important to the joy in your life, then you can often mitigate the stress by taking a good liver support supplement before bed. I'm a fan of Livaplex, by Standard Process.

If you're waking up frequently during the night to get up to pee, it's possible that your adrenals are over stressed and that they're having a hard time regulating electrolytes. For many people, the simple fix to this problem is to eat a few pinches of raw sea salt with some water right before bed. I don't recommend refined white salt because it can elevate the blood pressure.

If you think of yourself as an animal – as if you are your own pet – then you might be able to get a better sense of how to take care of yourself. If you have a pet that you care deeply about, you might learn about what that animal needs to thrive. You would make sure to feed that pet the right diet. Give it the right kind of shelter. If it's a terrarium pet, you might have lights that are set on a timer for the right times. You would keep its environment at the right temperature and/or pH if it's an aquatic pet.

I remember living with my first husband, who was crazy about Chinese water dragons. He had a pair for almost 20 years. This was quite a feat, seeing as their average life span is between 10 and 15 years! He had their vita-lights on timers set to optimize the ideal amount of sunlight that they would need. He made sure that they always had plenty of clean fresh water, hot rocks – but not too hot – for lounging on. He made sure that their environment was stimulating enough to keep their interest, but quiet enough to be relaxing. And they always got the best and highest quality food!

If you looked inside of our refrigerator, you'd think that we were health nuts. There was a rich array of organic kale, collard greens and assorted vegetables. The thing was, none of this food was for us. It was all for the various household reptiles. My ex took incredible care of these animals, and as a result, they lived an unusually long and healthy life! But as for himself? Well, he smoked like a chimney (about a pack of Winston Light 100s a day). He somehow figured that these were both "healthier" on account of being "light" and a better deal on account of being slightly longer than regulars. He ate at Taco Bell "to save money," drank heavily, barely slept and was in a constant state of stress and anxiety. He died of a heart attack at the ripe old age of 44.

Toxicity is the other side of the biochemistry coin. Nutrition can be thought of as things that should be going into your body, and toxicity comes from things that shouldn't be going into your body. Some sources of toxicity are obvious. Asbestos should not be going into your lungs. Lead should not be going into your skin (or into your drinking water). Sewage should not be mixed in with your drinking water. Most of us don't suffer from these big obvious sources of toxicity. Rather, we are likely experiencing the effects of a lifetime's worth of tiny bits of toxicity accumulated from thousands of sources.

A recent UCSF toxicity study on pregnant women detected 109 chemicals, including 55 never before reported in people and 42 "mystery chemicals," whose sources and uses are unknown. Almost half of these chemicals came from plastics, while the others came from cosmetics, household cleaners, personal care products, pharmaceuticals, flame retardants, pesticides and PFAs, which are used in carpets and upholstery.

We can't escape toxicity.

Even my friends who have moved far away into rural areas still encounter plenty of toxicity. Some of it is rather unexpected. A friend who moved up into a rural area of northern California was surprised to learn that the well water on her beautiful property was not safe to drink. It was contaminated – still! – from the aggressive mining activities that had gone on in the area more than 100 years ago, during the Gold Rush!

You can't escape it, but you have to become aware of it and mitigate it as best you can. Because you can always do better. And better **is** better! When you're young, it's easy to shrug and say, "We're all gonna die anyway so who cares?" But as you get older, you realize that there are good ways to die and bad ways to die. Good ways to get old and bad ways to get old. Slow poisoning is a terrible way to get old, and the kinds of deaths that are linked to excess toxicity are all horrible ways to die.

When we think of about toxicity and what organs handle detox, we often think of the liver. BJ Palmer, the developer of chiropractic had a funny saying. He said, "Is life worth living? That depends on the liver!" I love the play on words! Did he mean that it depends on the person doing the living? Or that it depends on the health of the liver?

In Chinese medicine, one of the emotions that goes with the liver is depression. Certainly, if the liver is in bad shape, people very often present with depression. This is not only a Chinese medicine correlation. Our own word "galled" meaning "shocked and angry" is also associated with the gallbladder and the bile, which is manufactured in the liver!

The liver is an incredible organ with hundreds of functions. We think of it mainly as the detox center of the body. But it's involved with allergies, viral conditions, sugar handling, fat metabolism, cholesterol synthesis and many other things. An unhealthy liver will also manifest in external ways, including muscle pain and tension between the shoulder blades, right shoulder blade pain, TMJ problems or skin and eye problems.

Reducing the toxic stress on the liver includes the obvious, such as reducing your alcohol and drug intake. But more and more people who don't even drink alcohol or take drugs are developing liver problems such as fatty liver. What's up with that? This can happen if you are just too much of a sugar-holic. You might not even think of yourself as a sugar-holic, but if you eat enough breads and pasta, then this can cause the same thing. Too many simple and refined carbohydrates can harm the liver. There's just no getting around it. No point in beating yourself up if you're gotten there – just work to turn it around.

As for drugs, you may think that you don't do drugs, but even over-the-counter medicines can harm the liver. The worst offender is one of the most common and seemingly harmless of them all: acetaminophen, aka Tylenol.

When I was around 18 or 19, my mom took me to a Korean traditional healer to help me with my chronic headaches. He did a short assessment (which seemed like magic) and looked at me sternly and asked about my drug use! At the time, I hadn't even tried any illicit drugs – not even a single puff of pot!

I told him, "Nothing!"

I wasn't on any prescription drugs, either. But... I did have a lifelong history of using Tylenol, Sudafed and other household medications for my frequent sinus headaches. Occasionally, I would take something stronger that my mom, a nurse, had probably smuggled home from work. From that time on, whenever I would visit a holistic doctor or practitioner, the topic of my liver would usually come up. And the questions about suspected previous drug use.

My conclusion is that it was the years of Tylenol. Also maybe the years of sugarholica and bread eating. As a skinny kid, I always thought that sugar and excess calories were only a problem for the fat kids. If you didn't get fat, then there was no problem! Little did I know that my metabolism may have hid the outward signs, but my liver was working way too hard. I used to eat entire boxes of mac and cheese in a single sitting or an entire loaf of Italian bread while sitting in the basement watching Dr. Who! Oh, to have a TARDIS and to be able to smack around one's younger self...!

I recommend caution when approaching the topic of toxicity and detoxification. There are a lot of scammers out there. There are also well-meaning but misinformed people selling services and items that purport to "detoxify" the body. Proceed with caution. Make sure that you have some kind of legit measurement that you can check in with to see whether or not something is delivering the goods. Is it really detoxifying? For our purposes, keep it simple and just start paying attention to where the toxins are coming from. As you are breathing things, touching things, ingesting things, think, "Does this belong in my body? No? Well how can I mitigate it?" Keep it real simple.

You need to support the organs that handle the cleanup. That would be the liver, the kidneys, the lungs and the large intestine. All of those organs will love you back if you stay nice and hydrated. Drink plenty of water! All of those organs will love you if you eat plenty of vegetables. All of those organs are happy if you're getting plenty of aerobic exercise. All of those organs appreciate a good night's sleep. Strive for clean air, clean water, clean food, exercise, good sleep. The rest is gravy.

Spirituality

The final S in our good S.E.C.S. formula stands for spirituality. Spirituality does not equate with religion, and an atheist can have just as rich of a spiritual life as any self-proclaimed "spiritual" person. When I think of the "spirit," I'm not thinking of a ghostly entity with a life separate from your own. I think of the spirit as that internal spark that everybody has. It's the thing that lights up when you feel profound joy and wonder. It pings when you get the feeling that you are part of something much bigger than yourself. It's impossible to feel completely at peace and comfortable in your own skin without satisfying this deep inner need.

Recent fMRI research confirms that there is even a specific place in the brain - the nucleus accumbens - that activates when one is having a powerful "spiritual" experience. Some people have run with this ball and claimed that it is "proof of God." I don't think that this is the case at all. The only thing it means is that there was – and probably is - some kind of survival advantage to having this feature. If we are designed to feel good when we use this feature, then we'll feel a lot better if we use it. Just don't get fooled into believing that something must be the ultimate truth just because you got a feeling – even a profound feeling! – in your body.

Growing up, I was a deeply religious kid. I believed 100% in what I was taught at church. I believed that there was only one true faith and that it was mine. My catechism teacher taught me to appreciate how lucky I was to be born and raised in the *only* true faith! He said that almost everyone else in the world was going to Hell even if they were "good people." He said that if they were *really* good people – but not in the right church – that the best they could hope for was to go to Limbo, which was a place kind of like Heaven, except that God would not be there. Those people wouldn't go to Hell, because they didn't deserve eternal torment and suffering, but they didn't deserve to be in the presence of God, either.

I remember one evening, when I was around 11 years old, standing in church and feeling incredibly grateful to be a member of *the One True Church.* I stood there, just thinking, wow, I am so lucky. There are billions of people in the world. Billions of people have existed in the past. And less than 1% of them got to Heaven. Out of *all* the people who have ever lived,

I am one of the lucky few who even has a chance to get to Heaven. I am so lucky. What are the odds that I would be born into the *only* church that *God* recognizes as *the right one? What are the odds?* And that is when my mind first shifted to doubt. What are the odds, indeed? Suddenly, it didn't make much sense.

As I drifted further away from the dogma of that religion, I maintained a deep interest in spirituality. I explored different organized and free-range religions and discovered that many of them had something valuable to offer. Many of them also led down some kooky pathways. These days, I no longer believe in a personified "sky God." But I do believe that there is great value in cultivating a healthy spiritual life.

There is a wealth of hidden wisdom encoded into the religions of the ages. What it can unlock is unique to the individual. So I say, explore as you will. But keep it personal and beware the dangers of seeking to impose it on others! Nothing good ever comes from that.

A sense of wonder and the sense that one is connected to something much bigger than oneself – maybe even something infinite – certainly has evolutionary advantages! It can drive one to strive harder than they ever thought possible. It can cause one to face incredible odds. It can also foster deeper bonds and cohesion within communities that share the same beliefs. Unfortunately, when twisted into dogma and religion, it has also led to profound tragedies and centuries of warfare. Even now, there is too much suffering happening in the name of religion.

The bottom line is, you have a nucleus accumbens. To experience a rich life and deep comfort in your own skin, this is one of the areas that needs to be satisfied. Whether it lights up out in nature, or while in service to others, or during ritual or meditation, you need to find what lights yours up and run with it.

There is an easy spirit-nourishing magical moment that is available to every single one of us. It's called the sunrise. I see the sunrise almost every single day.

I wasn't always a "morning person." For the first half of my life, I considered myself to be a night owl. In fact, my very first practice, in Atlanta, was a "night chiropractic" office! I thought, what a great niche! Nobody is open at night! I will cater to the night owls!

My office hours were from 5 to 11pm, Monday through Friday. What did I learn from that experience? I learned that no matter what your hours are, people want to come in right when you open or right before you close. And no matter that time you close, someone is always trying to get in two minutes before closing time. They will always have some story about how they really couldn't make it any earlier! When you close at 11pm, it's rarely about the traffic. Instead, it's about not wanting to miss their 9pm show or something. People!

Around 2018, a personal crisis reverberated into my business, which of course triggered a business disaster. During that year, I thought for sure that I would get squeezed out of my beloved San Francisco. My business seemed to be collapsing, and many of my clients were moving away – far away – to more affordable cities and states.

I own a little house in Sacramento, so I figured that's where I would have to go. Sacramento is OK, but my heart ached when I thought about being so far inland. I love the ocean. And yet, I hardly ever got to see it. I was always "too busy" to get to it, despite living just 3 miles away.

I decided that if I was going to have to leave, then I would make the most of my time left. I would go to the ocean every day. Even though it was just 3 miles away, getting out there and back still took over an hour round trip on the train or bus. Where would I find an extra 2 hours in my day? The only open spot was in the morning, before work.

So, I mapped out my day. If I woke up at 5am, then I would have enough time to catch the 5:30am L Taraval train to Ocean Beach. I would get to the beach by 6am. Then, I could walk along the shore for 1.5 miles, to Judah Street. I could catch the N Judah train back downtown to Van Ness station. And I'd be back in the office in time to see my first patient at 8:30am!

I know, it sounds crazy. It was really hard the first day. My body was like, WTF are we doing? But the payoff was so worth it. I practically had the beach to myself!

It was so beautiful. It was the end of June, so the sun had already risen by the time I got there. It was sunny and gorgeous. I had never seen Ocean Beach so sunny and so empty! The only other people out there were the earliest of the early bird surfers and a couple of joggers.

The walk was invigorating. New energy charged the rest of my day. I thought, that was awesome. I am definitely doing that again tomorrow.

The next day, it was as magical as the day before. But the ocean was different this time. The tide was a little different, and this time, there were a lot more sand dollars revealed on the beach! I picked some of them up to dry out at home. There were a few different birds. The clouds were different.

That day, too, was charged with a new energy. I thought, that, too, was awesome. I am definitely doing that again tomorrow.

I found that around 8pm, I started to hustle to wrap up my day so that I could be in bed by around 9! I needed to get enough sleep so that I could be rested for my big beach morning! Before I knew it, these beach walks became my favorite part of the day.

I went every single morning.

I used the train ride out to the beach as my journaling time. I used the train ride back from the beach as my time to mentally review my upcoming work day. Every single day at the beach was different. The tide was a little different every day. The waves were a little different every day. The birds, the shells, the distant boats, the surfers, the fishers – always something different.

Usually, it was all good, and sometimes there were tragedies. It's never a good thing when the rescue helicopter appears and makes passes back and forth over and over. You know they're looking for a body. And a few times a year, I'll find a dead sea lion, or even a dead baby deer, which is crazy. But even the dead things are kind of magical. It's that whole circle of life thing.

The ocean felt like my beautiful stylish girlfriend. I eagerly rushed to see what she would be wearing today. I kept up this daily routine until the trains stopped running about a month into the pandemic lockdown.

Over all that time, I experienced bright sunny summer mornings, cold foggy summer mornings, brilliant colorful sunrises, subtle twilights and the very spooky dark mornings of winter. Winter is terrifying out there, and on some of the high tide mornings, I walked mostly on the trail parallel to the beach. People say California doesn't really have seasons. But if you're outside every day paying attention, then you will experience the changes in the seasons!

The daily magic of those solitary morning beach walks infused my life with new energy and appreciation. Not surprisingly, my business came back to life! I could hear Dr. Scott's voice in my head. "When the doctor is down, the practice is down. When the doctor is up, the practice is up. "

I was getting such joy from my morning beach walks that I no longer felt bitter about the high cost of living in San Francisco. I finally felt that I was getting my money's worth! I no longer had the sinking feeling that I would have to leave. I felt that I belonged, and that I would be committed to serving this community – my San Francisco community – and being a part of it.

Not everyone can go to the ocean to watch the sunrise, but everyone can watch the sunrise, and it's beautiful no matter where you are. There's a magical peace about it. You can go to any ordinarily busy or crowded place, and at dawn, it's all yours.

The morning is the most productive time of the day. By the time I start seeing patients, I've already had a great day. This has been a real game-changer for me. Before starting my magical morning beach walk routine, Hal Elrod's *Miracle Morning* book changed my life. If you're not a "morning person" but are open to the idea of how becoming one can transform your life, check it out!

I share pictures from my morning beach walks on my personal Instagram, which is _kimakoi_.

Once you start to feed your spirit and see and feel more of the magic in your own life, the next thing to do is to share the magic! I like to think of sharing the magic as a revolutionary punk rock act.

Some people think of punk rock and revolution as smashing shit up and breaking things. I think of it as fighting against tyranny and oppression. And what is more tyrannical and oppressive than the sad mundane feeling that there's no magic in the world? That life is shit, that people suck, and that nothing good or interesting ever happens to you?

Well, in my tiny ways of sharing my own magic with other people, I feel like I am saying, "Take THAT, Universe!" There are lots of ways to do it. You will have to find ways that work for you. You can do Oprah style random acts of kindness in the world, such as paying the toll for the car behind you (harder to do now in California since they've done away with cash toll takers). Or you can discover your own personal magic to share.

Some of my chiropractic colleagues have taken a cue from Dr. John Hinwood and made little cards that simply say, "Expect a Miracle." They give them out to everyone they meet. It sounds cheesy, but it often brings a spark of joy to people! What does that even mean, to Expect a Miracle? Well, like everything, it means different things to different people. For some people, it is just the "sign" that they needed on that day to help them to keep on keeping on. It's a very simple and low-cost way to help a random stranger to feel better.

My main mode of random magic-spreading has been through my hobby of Postcrossing. (Shout out to rockstar San

Francisco bartenders Shirley Brooks and Matt Grippo for turning me on to this awesome addiction – er, hobby!)

Postcrossing, which I hope lasts forever, even though nothing lasts forever, is a postcard exchanging website. Once you register, you can receive up to five postal addresses of people from around the world. Then, you send them a postcard. Once they register your postcard as received, then you can request another address. You set up a profile that shares a bit about yourself and your interests. When you receive an address, then you also get to read the other person's profile and find out what they are interested in.

I love to try and find the perfect postcard for the other person! A lot of the time, it's nothing life changing. Some people just enjoy basic tourist postcards, and I send them my favorite San Francisco tourist cards. But sometimes, I can hit a real home run, and I get some pretty satisfying "thank you" messages in return! Here are a few examples of thank you messages that I have received from Postcrossers, just from sending some snail mail!

From Tatiana, in Russia:

"Hello Kim, this is an awesome postcard, especially the rabbit postage stamp! I was very tired and sad, and then I received your letter and was delighted. I think this is the point of Postcrossing. Thank you so much!"

From Dima, in Belarus:

"Hello and thousands of thanks to you for this perfect package!

I liked it very much from the moment when I've just saw it! It looked like a Christmas package and when I saw this creepy but also great postcard with Krampus on it it was perfect! I didn't know about this holiday. It was unknown for me, but now thanks to you I know it. I can't stop thanking you for these fabulous postcards, another one with San Francisco is brilliant too! This Soviet stamp on it was a kind of surprise for me! Thanks to you for all that you send me, for such great words on the postcards! Happy Postcrossing and merry Christmas! Great wishes from Belarus, Dima)"

From Patricie, in the Czech Republic:

"Hello K.!

Thanks for your Halloween postcard and your praise to my profile. :-)

San Fran! Pier 39, hippie district, Golden Gate, high hills, street train (forgot the proper word), Alcatraz and queer community! Yep, you're famous even in my little country. :-) If I'm goin' to hit the States one day, San Francisco is going to be my first stop. Screw New York!

Don't worry - every city could be bitchy sometimes (mine, for example, is the only one in our republic governed by Communist party - eeeew).

Wow, female-male ... So you are a Transformer! :-D World is so frakkin' awesome! Good for you! Nobody should be trapped in a body he doesn't like (trust me - I've been born with brown hair and wish to be ginger ever since!).

This is my 4th received postcard so far - 'till today I was written only by two boring German pensioners and creepy artist from Ukraine. Your letter is incarnation of my dream postcard! Funny, personal, interesting, warming. Thank you so so much! :-) And sorry for my transformer joke, if it was too much.

... Loving Richard Cheese and Lounge Against the Machine. Instantly. THANKS!

At the end you wrote "Sounds like you will be a great teacher one day." Well, I'm tryin my best. But, for the gazilionth time, thanks. :-)

Happy Postcrossing to you too, K.!" – from the Czech Republic

Once in a while, based on someone's hobbies or interests and the intersection with my own, I will be inspired to mail them more than just a postcard. Once, I received an address for a 50-something year-old man living in central Russia. In his entire life, he had NEVER SEEN THE OCEAN! This was unfathomable to me! How could someone live their whole life without ever seeing the ocean?!? He was just a working class guy in a small town in the middle of nowhere.

I am a big ocean fan and I am also quite rich in sand dollars and cockle shells.

So I decided to send him some of my shells in a little box along with the postcard. This little box blew his mind and was like a magical treasure received straight from the Universe! It felt like MAGIC and really made his day. And I felt really good and triumphant, too. For less than the cost of lunch, I made magic for someone on the other side of the world! Someone who I would never meet, but who would remember the magic and talk about it for a long time to come.

It also just tickles me to know that there are San Francisco sand dollars spreading joy all over the planet.

It's a very satisfying hobby. It feeds my soul, and it doesn't take much time. Maybe 10 or 15 minutes to knock out a postcard depending on how much thought is going into the message or the stamp choices. And it doesn't cost that much money. It's true that postage is always going higher – just went up to $1.30 to send a postcard internationally and $0.40 domestically. But really, in the grand scheme of things, it's not expensive considering the joy you can bring to someone else and to yourself.

As an Olympic class Introvert, I have always enjoyed making friends through the mail. Thanks to Postcrossing, I have made some great new friends, too, some of whom I have even met! I visited a Postcrossing friend when I went to Finland with my son a couple of years ago. As I type these words, I am wearing a pair of hand-knitted socks that a different Finnish Postcrossing friend made for me! I'm thinking of yet another Finnish Postcrosser friend who I'd like to visit next time I'm out there.

I dunno what it is about Finland... I just love it. Maybe it because Finland is considered an introvert country and a "5" country on the Enneagram, and I am a[n obviously] introverted 5. Maybe it's because my favorite guilty-pleasure band is the Finnish love-metal band HIM. Maybe it's because Finland has the best postage stamps of any country in the whole world! Whatever it is, I love it. It lights my fire.

Sharing the magic in your personal life gives you a rich feeling that is highly satisfying. You can bring the magic into your business and your professional life as well. As with your personal life, you will have to figure out for yourself what the most relevant and appropriate way for this would be. It doesn't have to be fancy.

Personally, I am also a big fan of rocks. I don't really believe that rocks have magical powers in and of themselves.

But I do believe that they can evoke ideas and feelings, and they do have their unique scientific properties, right?

One year, on Patient Appreciation Day, I had set aside a small rock in an envelope for each patient who was on the schedule. I also included a little Patient Appreciation card listing 3 things that I appreciated about each of those people. I added a small note listing some of the things that the enclosed rock traditionally symbolized.

I was surprised to find out years later that some of my patients still carried around those little rocks because they just made them feel good! They became little talismans and a source of personal magic. Sometimes just that little notecard with the top 3 things you like or appreciate about someone is enough to light them up. It can make their day or week a bit lighter than it would have been otherwise!

Chapter 4

The Issues are in the Tissues!

T he first time I really got that the body hid stress patterns was shortly after graduating from chiropractic school. I knew about "emotional stress" affecting the body. After all, I was no stranger to stress headaches and things like that. I knew that stress also made me sick sometimes. I could see that stress made other people sick, too. But I didn't think that my own body could be manifesting a stress that I was completely unaware of.

Towards the end of chiropractic school – during the last year or so – I developed a nagging pain in my mid-back. It was right between the shoulder blades. On a scale of 1-10, it was a 2 or 3. It wasn't bad, but it was almost always there. Dull.

Aching. It felt like something needed to 'pop.' The solution seemed simple enough. Get someone to pop it!

There was no shortage of eager fellow chiropractic students who offered to give it a go! But to no avail. No one could move that bone to give me any lasting relief. X-rays didn't reveal anything unusual about that area. When no students could help, I asked some of the teachers. No luck. After graduating, I went under the care of a well-known chiropractor in town. I hoped that he could help. While he did help with other things, nothing really helped that nagging point between my shoulder blades. Eventually, I gave up on it. I figured nobody's perfect, and that's just going to be one of my own imperfections.

One day, I was talking to one of the neighborhood chiropractors, and I mentioned the spot between my shoulder blades. I told him how no one had ever been able to help me with it.

He shrugged and said, "It's probably emotional."

I rolled my eyes.

"Great. Well how do I fix it?"

He told me to stick out my arm and resist against his pressure. What happened next just seemed weird. He was pushing my arm, which sometimes seemed to stay strong and sometimes seemed to go weak. He asked me to think about some different things while pushing my arm. It didn't make sense to me, but I went along with it.

He told me that according to my body, I was angry with my mom, but it went back to an incident much earlier in my life, around age 4. This was the age when I got the worst beating of my entire life. I didn't know what the beating at age 4 had to do with the current pain in my back. But I followed the directions, and put one hand on my forehead and the other hand over my liver area. I breathed deeply while imagining and feeling the anger surrounding that childhood beating.

While I breathed, Dr. Mike tapped me on the back. Then, he had me hold out my arm again. Strong.

"OK," he said, "Fixed it."

I moved around to see if I could find the pain between my shoulder blades. To my astonishment, it was gone! What just happened? I thought that maybe this was just a temporary power of suggestion. But it stuck. That nagging pain between my shoulder blades never came back. It really was some kind of stuck emotional thing!

"What was that??" I asked. That was NET. Neuro Emotional Technique.

In the 23 years since that first profound NET treatment, I can't even tell you how many times I am surprised by what my own body is hiding from me! Problems would seem to be coming from a logical structural or chemical cause. But then they would not resolve after following the corresponding logical care plan.

Then, as a last-ditch effort, I would check to see if it could be emotional. And then boom, it would resolve. Eventually, I would look sooner rather than later for an emotional component! But the body always surprises me. It's the nature of the beast.

My latest surprise came about two hours ago! With all the extra writing I've been doing lately, I seem to have developed some swelling in two fingers on my right hand. I thought it was just from overuse. Or maybe from a pinched nerve in my lower neck. Or maybe I've been eating badly during this busy time.

For whatever reason, I didn't check for emotional component until this morning. Well surprise surprise, my biofeedback indicators were pretty clear. There was a big stress component.

As I followed the biofeedback, it went to the feelings of grief and anguish. Grief and anguish about being completely clueless about the suffering of my little brother while we were young. I felt anguish about having been a terrible big sister. I wished that I could change the past. But of course the past is past. It's done.

I was not consciously aware that this was bothering me.

Why was my body thinking about that or reacting to it? Who knows? Sometimes it's a body memory thing. My brother's birthday is coming up, so maybe that's why. But once I became aware of the feeling, and then really felt the feeling while using the F.A.S.T. method, my body relaxed. The tightness in my fingers relaxed, too.

It's rare that any body problem or condition is 100% emotional. There are many factors that determine whether a certain body part will give you trouble. But often there will be a hidden emotional component that influences the healing. In the case of my fingers, I'm sure it would also help if I stretched my hands and my neck and improved my ergonomics while writing! But finding and clearing the hidden emotional component was a huge help.

These hidden emotional stresses can affect non-physical patterns as well. For example, around the same time as my first NET treatment, I was experiencing a frustrating pattern in my business. I was starting to see more patients, but I wasn't making any money! It seemed like everyone who walked in the door was either unable to pay, or the payment would be delayed by a long time.

There was the car accident case where I wouldn't get paid until all the treatment was done. There was the young worker from next door who had a complicated insurance plan that I wasn't sure would ever pay. There was the unemployed guy asking for sliding scale. And there were always various people asking for some kind of barter. Again, I told my woes to Dr. Mike and again, he said, "It's probably emotional. Hold out your arm."

This time, instead of just thinking about things, he had me say some things out loud while pressing my arm. "I'm OK with money." Boom – my arm dropped like a lead weight. He "cleared" a couple of things on being "OK" with money and receiving it, and within hours, cash started walking through the door.

First, a woman walked in.

"I saw your sign – do you take walk-ins and do you take cash?"

Then, a patient who didn't even have an appointment walked in with a friend.

"Hi – I was in the neighborhood and just wondered if I could get a quick adjustment. Also, could my friend get adjusted, too, and can I pay for her with cash?"

It seemed like a strange coincidence, and maybe it was. But after that treatment, the curse seemed to lift, and I no longer felt that I was attracting a steady stream of people who could not pay anything.

And how could I forget the biggest one of all? When I started out in that very first practice, I used to get a splitting headache and then have to go throw up if I saw more than five people a day!

I felt like that kid Kyle on South Park. He likes the girl, Wendy, but whenever she comes over and says "Hi" to him, he throws up! I liked seeing patients and I wanted to see more, but I, too, threw up when it really happened.

I only had about three months of survival cushion thanks to a business starter loan from my mom. I knew that I was in big trouble if this was going to happen to me whenever I saw more than five people on the schedule! Good old Dr. Mike once again came to the rescue. He did not seem alarmed at all when I told him my problem. It was the usual – hold up your arm and say, "I'm OK seeing more than five patients a day." This was a more complex problem, and we had quite a few layers to delve into, but we were able to clear it. And sure enough, it worked. I didn't have the barfy headaches anymore triggered by patient volume!

While the whole process seemed like magic to me at the time, it wasn't. Back then, when I was in my mid-20s, I still believed in a lot of woo. I thought that this might be a form of powerful "energy work," working on a mystical level as well as a physical level. Now I know that even though it felt magical, it was not magic.

The nervous system is incredibly powerful and complex, perfectly designed for human evolution. The thing is, over the last few thousand years – and especially over the last few hundred years and REALLY over the last 100 years – things have gotten... complicated.

We have learned to manipulate our environment. Our modern environments have become overwhelmingly complex. The nervous system can't take it all in. So, it has to select what the most important and relevant parts are. It's going to focus on the bits that seem most important to its own survival and safety. It doesn't matter what you want or what you think is logical or makes sense.

The nervous system is about stimulus and response. The responses are based on conditioning from the past. This is either your personal history and experiences or what's been encoded into your DNA.

Some people seem to magically attract money and business. Some people seem to magically repel it. Neither is magic. It's about what they are unconsciously seeking, and it operates through the nervous system. It's happening through the body, not through the woo.

When you are in business, especially when you're in business for yourself, your business is a reflection of your nervous system. Dr. Walker used to tell us, "Your practice is an exact replica of your nervous system." Want to know how you're doing? Look at your business. It's true, especially the smaller your business.

If you are disorganized and cluttered within your nervous system, then your practice or business will reflect that. If you are tired as hell, then your business will reflect that. If you are excited and energized, then your business will reflect that, too! In building our practices and businesses, Dr. Walker always placed a huge emphasis on getting ourselves "up."

When the doctor is down, the practice is down. When the doctor is up, the practice is up.

So, we had to get ourselves up. He said, you can't lose with this approach, because if you're up, then you're up! If your practice somehow doesn't go up, then it doesn't matter, because you're up! But of course, it will go up, because that's the way it works.

I was listening to a Mike Michalowicz podcast the other day with guest Jeffrey Shaw, the author of *The Self-Employed Life*. They were talking about how personal development and business development go hand in hand. This is especially true for self-employed people. Because when your business is basically YOU, then how you are showing up in the world is how the business is showing up as well. Taking care of your body is absolutely an important part of that self- and business development!

You cannot be "up" if your body is not along for the ride. Feeling good cannot happen without the cooperation of the body. What are feelings anyway? They're not abstract concepts within the mind. They are chemical reactions happening inside of the body.

Candace Pert, the late neuroscientist who discovered the opiate receptor and wrote the book *Molecules of Emotion*, also discovered that receptors for mood chemistry were located throughout the body – not just in the brain! You know this intuitively.

How do you even know if you are angry? You feel it in your body. You feel a tightening of the muscles of your jaw, a clenching of your fists, a fire in your belly or chest, and energy ready to burst. How do you know when you're sad? It might be the tears coming from your eyes, or the heavy feeling in your chest. How do you know when you're in love? It's the giddy light feeling in your body, maybe a fluttering in your heart.

What is the universal body experience of being terrified? People piss themselves. If you're nervous, your heart rate changes, you start sweating a little, your stomach may tighten, you may need to go to the bathroom. When you're excited, you feel a rush of energy. Your eyes brighten, your lungs may expand.

Without a corresponding physiology, there is no feeling. You become Spock-like and operate from logic, but feelings are in the body. And so if you are aspiring to feel "up" and to bring your business "up" then you have got to pay attention to your body and help it to help you.

Where your mind goes, energy flows. Whatever you pay attention to, you will see and experience more and more of it.

Once you discover or decide on what you really want and take serious action steps towards getting it, the body can resist in a big way. Especially if it is something you have never had before. Remember, the body doesn't care about whether you are "happy." It only cares that you are safe. And safe basically means surviving whatever it knows that you have survived in the past.

The body can use all sorts of tactics to get you to keep on keeping on with the old patterns. One of the simplest self-sabotaging methods it can use is to just make you sick.

My body used to pull this "getting sick" method every time I ever committed to a group social event. It would happen almost any time I committed to a purely social get-together (as opposed to a work seminar, etc.) involving more than four people. Invariably, a day or two before the event, I would get sick. My throat would get itchy, I would start to feel queasy, maybe even develop a fever and be sick enough to legitimately have to stay home from work. But almost at the start time of the event – once it became impossible for me to attend said event – I would begin to feel much better. Soon, I would be totally back to normal, feeling perfectly fine, within hours!

My body thought that by keeping me away from these social events, it was basically saving my life. I have since used the Neuro Emotional Technique method to clear some of those unhelpful patterns. Now I can just honestly say, "No thanks" to social events that I don't really want to go to, or "Yes" if I do, and I can make it there without my body sabotaging it! But the animal brain is crafty, and as we strive to move forward and get better and better, it will continue to resist whenever a new barrier is approached.

Recently, as I was working towards a new goal of living in my dream home, I could feel my body resist as I moved towards bolder action steps. I knew that these steps would get me out of my comfort zone, but closer to the goal. As I approached some new steps that I had never taken before, I was surprised to feel my body start to cry! Now this was a completely unexpected thing because I'm not a crier! But I could feel a sense of fear, hopelessness and anguish and I cried about it. I'm happy to report that I made it through that experience, and I'm editing this book right now sitting in said dream home!

Another way that the body can sabotage you while thinking that it's doing you a favor is to create severe pain syndromes, such as low back pain, sciatica, migraines, etc. Less than a year before graduating from chiropractic school, I read Dr. John Sarno's book *Healing back Pain*. Sarno was a New York orthopedist who believed that almost all back pain was really caused by deeply hidden unconscious rage. According to

Sarno, the body needed to create a distraction to protect you from some rage that it felt you couldn't handle. He believed that if you could discover what this hidden rage was really about, then the pain would simply disappear.

His theory was controversial, but thousands of people have found relief from their chronic pain by following his advice to stop all physical treatments and to focus simply on uncovering the source of their hidden rage. His book rocked my world and freaked me out. Was my new profession really a sham? Did I just get myself almost $100,000 into student loan debt for nothing?

In my panic, I wrote a letter to Dr. Sarno, explaining my conundrum. To my surprise, he wrote me back! He basically said that I seemed like a nice kid and that he wished me well, but that he held my profession in great disdain and yes, he did basically think that the whole profession was a sham.

I eventually concluded that Sarno's theory on chronic back pain was partially correct. Indeed, many cases of back pain and other chronic health conditions really are primarily rooted in unconscious emotional patterns. But hidden rage was only one of the possible emotions causing the problems, and there were many ways to uncover them beyond just trying to figure it out!

What complicated the matter, though, was that hidden emotional patterns didn't just come from our own stresses. We could literally inherit them from our parents and grandparents.

You have a unique heritage. Even in the most genetically homogenous groups, there is a rich heritage hidden in the DNA. And I can guarantee that most of the people reading this book are not from particularly homogenous DNA groups!

Not very long ago – just a couple of hundred years ago – the average human spent their entire life within about a 20 mile radius from the place of their birth. Can you imagine such a thing? And yet, that's the way it was. These days, the average person can travel that 20 miles in a single day. In their lifetimes, they may live hundreds or thousands of miles away from their place of birth. They may have kids with people from the other side of the planet! Our DNA heritage now tells complicated stories. They have unexpected impacts on our health, our minds and our lives!

I'm very interested in genealogy and family history. It's fascinating to me. But to my mom, not so much. Once, I was taking pictures of old family albums to build a digital archive. My mom looked over at me and, in her classic demotivational style, asked, "Why are you doing that? What a waste of time. Why do you care about people you've never met, who you have no connection to whatsoever? Those people are strangers to you. Who cares about them?"

For a second, I was self-conscious and ashamed. I thought, yeah, these people are strangers. Why do I care...? But then, aside from the purely historical interest – and there's nothing wrong with having an interest in history – I thought, these people are not strangers to me. These people are alive inside of my DNA. Some of my quirky crap comes from some of these people. They are probably more intimately connected to me than I even know.

Once, I took a mushroom trip where this concept became even clearer to me. Am I allowed to say that? Maybe by the time this book goes to print, mushrooms will be legal. I mean, they're practically legal in Oakland now, so, San Francisco can't be far behind.

In my experience, every mushroom trip comes with a "theme," but I can't choose the theme ahead of time. It just reveals itself when it happens. So this one time, the theme was the ancestors. At one point, I could see my ancestors, basically riding in a little roller coaster car through my bloodstream. They were inside of me! I thought, oh! This is how you achieve immortality! You live inside of your descendants, through the blood. The blood really is the life!

I saw the faces of my ancestors, sitting in that roller coaster car, looking around with wonder. They could never have imagined this world in their wildest dreams! They could never have imagined ME as the inheritor of their legacies. They could never have imagined sharing a roller coaster car with other ancestors from such diverse places. They were having a great time. At one point, one of my warrior ancestors from northern Europe looked at the knives in my kitchen, stuck to the magnetic knife strip on the wall.

"What a peaceful time you live in! Such tiny weapons!" He was incredulous and wished that he had had the luxury of living such a life of peace. It's funny how everything is so relative.

The diverse mix of the ancestors in our blood adds a certain richness and uniqueness to our lives and our potential for contribution to society. But it can also create confusing and conflicting tendencies and impulses within ourselves. Again, as animals, we pass certain information down through the genes to keep our offspring safe. But if we're living from different lineages with different ideas of what's safe and what's not safe, it can set us up for war with ourselves! While overcoming these conflicts can set us up for even bigger triumphs, the challenge is no joke.

In Korea, there's a saying, when you are having trouble in your life, "Blame the ancestors." This probably comes from an idea like karma or the idea of the son having to pay for the sins of the father. But in a very real way, we literally do inherit from the ancestors more than just the color of our eyes and skin. We also inherit things like personality traits, problem-solving tendencies, and aptitudes for specific skills.

There are crazy things hidden deep in our DNA that do not activate until the biological or environmental conditions are right. This became incredibly clear to me as I made my journey through the world of gender transition.

I identified as more male than female from a very young age. Probably since around four years old. But nothing prepared me for the shift in reality as my chemistry changed. I used to play a video game called Soul Reaver, where you could go from this world to a parallel world. The parallel world looked the same as the regular world – same buildings, geography, etc. - but the colors were off. There was a thin veil or something that differentiated it. I feel like that is kind of like the worlds between people who run on estrogen and people who run on testosterone. They're the same world, but... different.

Smells changed subtly.

Colors shifted. Especially red. Red became suddenly much more vivid than it had been before. It was very strange. When traffic lights turned red, I was startled at how bright they seemed! If a woman wore bright red lipstick, my eyes were drawn to it in a way that they had never been before! In fact, a lot of my perceptions about women changed. Things that I had thought were purely socialized behaviors started to become clear to me as biological impulses.

For example, while talking to women, I had a really hard time focusing on their eyes. I kept wanting to stare at their chests! Women would speak to me, and I would be thinking in my head, "Eye contact. Eye contact. Eye contact." I would sometimes have a hard time following the conversation because of how much energy was going into avoiding looking at her breasts!

I suddenly realized that men deserve more credit than they get for how much they do show restraint! It sounds misogynistic, and most women can hardly conceive of this. While straight women do indeed feel strong physical attraction to some men, they don't feel the urge at the same intensity. Trust me. I was a female-bodied person with a pretty darn healthy libido back in the day. And I never had to mentally struggle with the urge to not stare at a guy's package while talking to him!

Also, like clockwork, three days after my weekly shot, when my body testosterone hit its peak, I felt a weird impulse to be hostile towards women! At first, I thought this was a fluke. But the pattern persisted. It's disturbing and fascinating at the same time.

To me, it wasn't a mystery as to where this aggro macho man tendency came from.

It was from the ancestors!

The male side of my lineage was a long line of soldiers, as far back as we could trace. It was soldiers and sailors dating back to the Revolutionary War and beyond. Them there's fighting genes! On the Korean side, as far as I knew, I basically came from a line of peasant migrant workers. They had no known family tree extending beyond the living memory of my mom, now that my grandparents are dead. Their families were originally from the northern part of Korea, so, whoever was left behind is likely long dead. So, who knows the true history?

Anyway, this reptile brain has survived generations upon generations of wars and shady humanity. It doesn't give up without a fight, and it will remember the most crucial of survival skills for a long long time!

So, these ancestors live inside of you. They influence you and, in some ways, run you without your even knowing it. You've got to make friends with them if you are going to move forward in success as a unit! How do you make friends with the ancestors? Through your body.

Food is a big component. What kind of food did your ancestors thrive on? This is not just about adopting a "paleo" diet because "that's what cave people ate." This is more nuanced and individualized.

Take the whole dairy thing, for example. Most people in the world don't do well with cow's milk. Almost all people of African descent are lactose intolerant or dairy sensitive. People of Asian descent tend to not do that great with it, either. But white Europeans often do just fine with it! In fact, many of them thrive on cow dairy products. This is because their ancestors have been consuming it for a long time.

Likewise, some people want very much to follow a vegan diet for health or philosophical reasons, but their bodies are not that into it. They're not really designed for it. Whereas some people of Indian descent do great on vegetarian diets because their ancestors have been following that diet for many generations.

Your ancestral heritage might be complicated. More people than ever are of mixed racial heritage. You have to be honest with yourself and take a good look at your heritage and most of all, listen to your body. There are some general guidelines that are helpful in figuring out what kinds of foods will be helpful versus what kinds will not.

After years of practice, I have noticed that people generally do pretty well with the "blood type diet" approach. The blood type diet was popularized in the 1990s by Peter D'Adamo. At first, I thought that this sounded like complete crap. Why would it matter what blood type you are? But upon closer inspection, it does make sense. People with different blood types have different enough biochemistry that they can't receive blood from other types. (Other than AB+, who can receive blood from any other Rh+ blood type). Moms who are Rh- have to be monitored very closely if they are carrying a baby with Rh+ blood otherwise big problems can happen during the birth!

I'm a person with A+ blood. That means that I'm basically supposed to follow a mostly vegetarian type of diet with mainly fish for the animal protein. I was not happy to learn this information. I wanted to be a meat eater. Me think meat taste good! The pescatarian life sounded boring to me. But, if I'm completely honest with myself, the truth is that I do tend to feel better if I follow a mostly vegetarian diet.

I more easily maintain a healthy weight, healthy blood sugars numbers, etc., if I do follow a pescatarian diet. When D'Adamo's *Phenotype Diet* book came out, I was hoping for a different outcome. It was a more nuanced approach to the blood type diet. I eagerly read the book, hoping to magically land in the group of the meat eaters! Nope, my recommended diet was basically the same as before. Damn. What a waste of a book. I have read other similar books, too, in the hopes of discovering that I am some kind of really special A+ blood person who can thrive on meat, but now I've stopped. There's no escaping my basic DNA.

When I transitioned hormonally to male, I did suddenly develop a higher tolerance for meat and dairy. I attributed this to a sudden activation of more of my northern European genes, from my dad's side of the family. Testosterone caused me to lose hair like my dad – on my head, unfortunately – and to gain hair on my back! As I developed more of those hairy Anglo guy qualities, it made sense that my body would do better with those kinds of foods.

Aside from eating the foods of your ancestors, how else can you honor them and help your body to feel good and satisfied in alignment with your people? Gardening, digging in the dirt, using your hands to construct things, riding horses, sailing, hiking... there are any number of things that your ancestors may have done that can bring you a deep sense of satisfaction that you don't even understand. When you find it, it's a healthy thing to nourish. It doesn't have to be logical. Remember, this is all unconscious stuff, buried deep in the recesses of your DNA. But the more you can be in alignment with your whole self, the more you can live a satisfying life that also feels magical!

Speaking of magical, some people like to practice ceremonial and ritual traditions that honor the ancestors. This isn't really the book for that, but I believe that there is real value in ritual. I don't believe in superstition. But we are living with nervous systems that have evolved over thousands and thousands of years with ritual as an important part of daily life.

Recent studies have even shown that completely meaningless secular rituals have a measurable effect on us. They can be used for goal setting and habit changing.

In a 2018 study entitled *Enacting Rituals to Improve Self-Control* (published in the Journal of Personality and Social Psychology), researchers found that even secular rituals – ritualized gestures with no religious or other meaning attached to them – were useful to improve self-control. For example, in one of the experiments, participants were instructed to cut their calories by 10%, cut the food on their plate into small pieces, rearrange the pieces so that they were symmetrically on the plate, and then press the eating utensil onto the food three times. The ritual had no inherent meaning, but the study found that the group performing the ritual was better able to change their habits towards healthy eating than the control group. The hypothesis was tested using six different experiments, and the conclusions were the same: rituals can have beneficial consequences for self-control.

Maybe someday, the parts of the brain that respond to ritual will evolve out of existence. But that's a long way off. Right now, for you and me, we have brains that do respond to ritual. If you want to be one of the people who adds to the generations upon generations that it will take to extinguish it, hey, go for it. But for myself, I'm going to take advantage of it and go with it! You don't have to join a cult. I mean, I did, by accident, but that's another story for another book.

Traveling is also a great way to connect with the ancestors. Travel is awesome anyway – you don't need to twist my arm to get me to travel! But there's something powerful about visiting the place where your ancestors, recent or distant, are from. Breathing the air. Touching the ground and the rocks.

Walking through the oldest parts of the town. It helps to bring you closer to yourself in another way.

One of the most powerful ways to connect with the ancestors is to make great-great-great-great-great-great-great grandma and grandpa proud. How do you do that? You can do that by living your best life and conquering *their* fears for themselves and their offspring. You can do this by acknowledging and enjoying your safety, your shelter and the fact that you live in a time and place where food and water are abundant. I mean, clean water – hot and cold! – comes out of a TAP! We have flush toilets! We can order food and beverages of all kinds to be delivered right to our doors! It's more than a little amazing.

If you've been in business for any length of time, you know that people do not make purchase decisions through logic. People make most of their decisions based on their emotions. You may have the greatest product or service, but if you do not connect with your customers on that emotional level, then business will suffer. While some people are good at faking, thus the phrase "Fake it 'til you make it," the truth is, nobody can really fake it all the time.

Even the most clueless customer can pick up on subtle cues. Everybody's body is way smarter that we think it is. If your body is low energy, your skin and eyes are dull, your voice is unenthusiastic, then you will relay this low-energy impression to your customer.

If your mind is sluggish and you can't focus, you keep dropping the ball. This will invariably hurt sales and relationships with the customers.

If you are constantly in pain or having a hard time moving, you can't be laser focused on your client and their needs. If in the back of your mind you are constantly worried about yourself, how can you be attuned to the needs of your business?

I remember back when I was pregnant, at one point, I developed a terrible case of pregnancy sciatica. It was mortifying. Here I was, a chiropractor, and I was having debilitating sciatica! I gritted my teeth and walked slowly in my office, hoping that no one would ask why I was walking slower than usual. Mercifully, in my job, most of my clients were face down for most of the treatment, so they couldn't see me limping around the table! I thought I was doing a great job of hiding my discomfort, but I'm sure it affected my practice on some level. Those were not the greatest times in my practice. Indeed, the high points of my business life were the times when I was taking the best care of my body as well as my mind.

What you believe really does determine what you experience. Really. The meaning that we place on experiences have a huge impact on how we are influenced by them. Even experiences that could be said to be universally bad, such as getting smacked across the face, can have a wide range of meanings attached to them. They can leave different lasting impressions or none at all!

For example, imagine that a child is slapped across the face by an adult in front of other children. It can be physically painful, deeply humiliating and psychologically scarring. But what if the child is slapped across the face as part of a traditional ritual marking the transition to adulthood? Then the same painful experience can become a source of pride. It can become a shared memory and positive bonding experience with the group.

Context is everything.

People can suffer tremendously when there seems to be "nothing going on." Or they can experience bliss when it seems like they should be suffering. We don't have to be mystics or saints to experience positive feelings more often than negative, but we do need to make a conscious decision to do so. Our unconscious programming has been negative, for the most part. So while at first it may feel fake, we have to work to lay down those new neural pathways!

In the NET (Neuro Emotional Technique) world, we talk a lot about the concept of emotional reality. This is the idea that people tend to experience reality through the lens of their own emotional experiences.

What someone has experienced as fully real and true is often not what was going on in objective reality. Over the years, I have had many clients come in with extreme trauma stemming from medical crises experienced as little kids, babies and even as fetuses! How could a fetus experience and remember trauma?

Remember, the younger you are, the more rapidly your cells are dividing and the bigger the impact of environmental factors. This is why certain drugs taken at key points in pregnancy can cause lifetime malformations. In one particularly memorable case of lasting anxiety stemming from in utero stress, a patient of mine was originally "diagnosed" as being a tumor rather than a baby! For a significant portion of the pregnancy, their mom thought that they were a tumor.

The medical conversations happening were all about how to kill or get rid of the tumor. Imagine, even if you don't understand language, the difference between living inside of a being who loves you and thinks you're a precious little baby versus living inside of a being who thinks that you are a tumor and should die! Some of my patients were born as preemies and experienced trauma from the body memories of being inside of the incubator, separate from their mom and from anyone else.

One patient said that he even has dim memories of being inside of that little box and hearing the cries of the other babies in the room. Even though he couldn't see them, he knew that there was something wrong about how he was inside of this encasement, but the other babies were out in the open somewhere. Not knowing the reality of the life-saving treatments, the emotional reality was the experience of being wrongfully singled out and punished. The babies and little children in the hospital were, in fact, loved by their parents, but that was not their experienced emotional reality.

And so the nervous system runs with the emotional reality and makes future decisions based on it. A former preemie, traumatized, might grow up to have a constant desire to be strong and to prove that they are strong. A baby born with the impression of being unwanted – such as an "oops" baby – might strive to constantly prove how useful they are to their parents. Sometimes the emotional reality drives people to "positive" outcomes, and sometimes it drives people to repeat unhealthy patterns over and over.

Emotional realities can be profound and life-changing, as with medical traumas early in life. But they can also be more mundane and show up in our day-to-day life. A large stick on the hiking trail after rounding a sharp corner can cause a startle when you think it's a big snake! More subtle instances of emotional reality happen all the time every day. Perhaps the most common of all is when we get into "mind reading." Of course, nobody can really read anybody else's mind, but we do it all the time. We decide what someone else is thinking or feeling. Especially when we think it's about us. We make decisions and act accordingly. While we may get it right once in a while, the fact is, we are almost always wrong. In fact, we are so close to "almost always" wrong that I may as well just say "we are always wrong."

There is a great therapeutic system, designed for group therapy, called Systems Centered Therapy. In this system, they have a nice practice surrounding this mind reading tendency. In it, people are encouraged to speak up when they catch themselves thinking that they know what someone else is thinking. If the other person is around, they say, "I'm having a mind read that you are thinking ___. Is that accurate?"

Of course, the answer is usually no, it's not. But it's a nice way of asking, which does not put the other person on the defensive, and it doesn't become accusatory. It's great, and it would be nice if this concept of "checking in with a mind read" found its way into our culture.

So, memory is a crazy thing. We think of our memories as video recorders. They are not! We think that if there is a gap in our memories, it's as if the recorder wasn't recording. Memory is a lot more complicated than that, and it's a lot more inaccurate than that, too.

When I was around 14 years old, I decided to do a memory experiment, to see if I could create a false memory in myself. I was out on one of my middle-of-the-night mini expeditions with my friends Joey and Ryck. We were hanging out in Joey's mom's car, which of course he had stolen for the night. I can't remember if he even had a driver's license yet. Probably not. Anyway, we were sitting in the car, listening to music, and I was looking at the trees lining the parking lot. I thought, I wonder if I can make a fake memory. I wonder if I can imagine there are creepy people sitting up in those trees. I wonder if I will remember creepy people in the trees when I remember this night. After all, I theorized, memories are internal images in your imagination from something that doesn't exist anymore. So if I use my imagination at the same time that I'm making a memory, I wonder if the future memory will mix them all together? I wonder. So I kept looking at the trees and imagining creepy pale alien faces looking back at me.

And you know what? It worked!

Whenever I think back to that night, I can see Ryck, Joey, the car, the parking lot, the trees... and the creepy alien-like people in sitting in the trees staring at us! So this was me deliberately making a fake memory. But how many times are we distracted, or thinking intently about something else while something is happening in the present? Do you think this affects memory? Emotional life? I say yes.

Bruce Lipton wrote a great book called *The Biology of Belief*. He talks a lot about epigenetics. This is the study of how external factors – including nutrition and emotional conditions – can change our DNA. It's a fascinating read and a fascinating field!

There is evidence that psychological trauma and anxiety can pass down the DNA for three generations. That means that if you had a great life and your parent had a great life, but your grandparent had a traumatic life, guess what? YOU can still experience inherited trauma and anxiety.

At first, it sounds too fantastical to be real. How could emotional trauma change our DNA and linger for generations?

But it totally makes sense when you remember that we are animals.

How do animals pass on information about danger? Whether it's dangerous foods, predators, etc., how do baby animals learn without school? Some baby animals spend some time with their mothers, but some baby animals are totally on their own right from the get-go! How do they learn?

As a religious, kid, I was told that God just made it so. Animals had no free will, so they are just pre-programmed to live a certain way. But humans have free will, so we can do anything, and we have to learn how to live. That's why we need schools and churches. That's what I was taught, anyway.

Well, not true. There are some neurologists that believe that humans *don't* have free will (any more than other animals). They are fairly certain that we are just behaving off of stimulus and response. It just seems like free will because there are so many different stimuli and responses that they can seem random. Also, our brains are constantly making up stories about why we just did what we did. I meant to do that. I chose to do that. But really? Maybe we just did it.

Again, remember, we are animals. *We **are** animals!*

How does a baby turkey know that a rattlesnake is bad news? Because its ancestors – the ones who survived rattlesnake encounters – knew that they were bad news. The information was somehow encoded into the DNA. It happened with enough regularity over time that it was reinforced. And now, no baby turkey needs to be taught that these snakes are danger noodles of the highest order! Most animals instinctively know what foods they need to eat and which things they don't. This information has been reinforced for generations upon generations. It often doesn't really need to be taught.

So, it's no wonder how we can already have predispositions to certain anxieties and fears, based on generations of animal data. I believe that this is part of where racism comes from. Sure, there is some degree of being taught by example to treat others with kindness or with derision. But after generations of enmity against certain people, of course people are going to be born with certain tendencies. It's literally in the blood.

As a child of mixed race, I never really understood white supremacists. I understood racism, sort of, as I realized that I, too, was prejudiced against certain people. I was even a bit prejudiced against myself. I was not as proud of my Korean heritage as I was of my British heritage. This was true even though the British part of my heritage was so distant that no one in my family could even tell me which parts of England, Scotland or Ireland "our people" were from! All we had was the last name – McCaughey – which itself had been altered over the years.

I never understood the white supremacists until the day that I visited my aunt in Korea, on an American army base. I had never seen so many mixed race (specifically ½ Korean) kids in one place in my entire life! I immediately thought, "Oh my god, THIS is my 'country.' THIS is where I'm supposed to go when people yell, 'go back to where you came from!' All of those strange feelings rushed in, and then, I felt a sudden and unexpected surge of pride. Racial pride! Something in my brain said, "YOU ARE THE MASTER RACE. SEE? HERE ARE YOUR PEOPLE. THE REAL PEOPLE!"

And finally, I got it.

The white supremacy thing (or the any supremacy or racial pride thing) was an animal reaction. A biological reaction. It probably didn't have that much to do with ideology. Ultimately, it was straight up biology.

From that point on, I jokingly called myself a "Halfie supremacist." It was sort of a joke, but it sort of wasn't. I "happened to" mainly date other people of mixed race, and I ultimately married and had a baby with another half Korean! We joked (but it wasn't a joke – it was true) that when a ½ Korean mates with another ½ Korean, they produce another ½ Korean. It was a weird source of pride.

The fact that we are animals is why so much information about safety and danger gets passed down through the DNA. It's why much of it seems messed up and irrelevant thanks to our extreme manipulation of our environments over the millennia!

For hundreds of thousands of years, the threats to a small human's life were about the same as the threats to a big human's life. Dangers like animals with sharp teeth, poisonous plants, lightning, fire, falls from great heights. Stuff like that!

But as we become more and more complicated and our lives become more complicated, so does the data that is passed epigenetically. Traumatic wartime experiences of past generations made imprints in the DNA. That DNA was passed on to their children and grandchildren. In recent times, we have experienced some relatively cushy lives, compared to the hardships of times past. And maybe our parents had relatively cush lives. But what about their parents, and their parents?

My mom was a North Korean refugee in the early 1950s. She was almost abandoned on the side of the road as a 2-year old. My grandmother carried her on her back, heading on foot to the safety of the south. Other people running past her encouraged her to ditch my mom. They said, "leave the kid behind! She's only a girl anyway!" Mom remembers seeing little babies and small kids abandoned along the side of the road. Incredibly traumatic time! They had to hide in the woods for days, where my great-grandmother packed her wounds using pine sap and tree leaves to stop the bleeding. She had been shot twice by North Korean soldiers while running across the border.

In our modern environment, there are countless artificial stimuli that can freak out a baby or a small child. But these may have nothing whatsoever to do with averting trouble as an adult. A baby can have a traumatic experience in the hospital from a difficult or premature birth, surgery, etc. and then later have an aversion to all doctors and medical environments. This can be true even though they have no conscious memory of the initial experience.

So, what does this have to do with business? It has everything to do with how you are *experiencing* your business. It has to do with how your business shifts to fit into the story that your animal body has created. You brain is constantly seeking patterns and placing meaning onto them. This was all part of the original survival mechanism. But again, in the modern world, there are countless items for the brain to choose from.

You have your own unique experiences, conditioning, and genetic tendencies. Based on these, your brain will cobble together a story that is unique to you. You will perceive it as "fact" and "reality" but it's really quite pliable and may as well be an alternate reality of your own choosing!

In business, you may think that many things are completely out of your control. The economy. The competition. The timing. These things may indeed have some impact on your business. However, the brain can override any and all of these things to various degrees, no matter what. Nobody can succeed without their brain being on board. It may seem like some people are "just lucky." If you dig deeper, you will discover that almost all successful people use very similar methods to become successful. Their brains are calibrated for success, whether intentionally or not.

I read a lot of memoirs. Almost immediately upon starting on testosterone, I entered my 2nd puberty. This time, I was experiencing it as a teenage boy. One of my male friends had warned me, "You are going to be sooo horny." I thought, theoretically, this was likely to be true. I halfway doubted it, though, because my libido had been in a dead zone for almost four years, ever since giving birth to my son. My body had never really recovered from that, and I doubted if I would ever have an appetite for sex again.

Well, hello testosterone! Indeed, as my friend predicted, I was horny all the time. I mean, allllll the time. My sexuality shifted, and suddenly I was strongly attracted to women. While I had never been that into porn before, I suddenly became really interested in it. And just like a teenage boy from the 80s or 90s would have loved to do, I subscribed to Hustler magazine. The budding testosterone-fueled teenager in me was all about the pictures and the free DVD that came with each issue! But, I kid you not, I also really enjoyed the articles!

I almost laughed out loud as I was reading and thinking, "these articles are really good!" No woman would have believed a man who said, "I read it for the articles," but... lo and behold.

I subscribed for about two years. Until the ridiculous teenager phase of the hormonal shift wore off and the pile of bonus DVDs was growing to an embarrassing level. What was the point of that digression? Oh, it was during that time that I read *How to Make Love Like a Porn Star: A Cautionary Tale*, the memoir of porn star Jenna Jameson.

Everybody (other than people who work in the industry) thinks that porn stars have an easy life. How hard could it be to basically just have sex on camera? Well, like any real job, it's not that simple or easy. I was surprised (though I shouldn't have been) to read about how Jenna worked hard and went above and beyond what her colleagues were doing. She worked on her mindset, trained and rehearsed during her off days, networked, marketed – all sorts of very mundane business things. It was fascinating, and I really enjoyed reading the book!

The point is that success has only a little to do with luck. Sure, luck helps – everyone would love a lucky break – but luck favors the prepared. It always takes **action**. There is a great West African proverb that says, "When you pray, move your feet." My mentor, Dr. Scott Walker, used to say, "The Universe rewards the action step." He later amended this to, "The Universe *only* rewards the action step." Passive will not cut the mustard.

And if you can bring your body on board, then all the better! Because most of the things you do are unconscious. If you can train your unconscious body to move in the direction that you prefer, then that is the best thing of all. Remember, the thinking brain, the neocortex, is the last to know anything. It thinks it's in control, but it's not. If you can get the larger beast below you to move in the direction you want to go, then you're good as gold.

Chapter 5

Comfortable

To be comfortable in your own skin you need to make friends with your body. This is so important. Everyone is like "love yourself!" Yes, that is pretty important. But that is easier said than done. How do you even do that?

I say the most important step is to **STOP JUDGING YOUR BODY**.

It's one thing to constantly strive to improve yourself – that's a lifelong journey. But the judgement is completely counterproductive. Nothing great comes of it, and it doesn't mean anything anyway. First of all, there's nothing "wrong with" your body. Second of all, we've already established that your thinking brain doesn't know doodly squat about what your body is actually up to and why.

Your body is an incredible thing. It's almost like its own planet or galaxy, supporting many tiny civilizations and ecosystems within it. Give up the thought that you and your puny thinking brain could even begin to conceive of what's going on in there. We'd be dead in a second if we handed the reins of our physiological functioning over to our thinking brain!

Even if it's treating you badly, marvel at the complexity and evolutionary wonder of your body. Even if it's hurting or malfunctioning, it's still incredible. *One of the biggest keys to success is to feel comfortable in your own skin.*

One exercise that I have found to be really helpful is to step outside of yourself and to pretend that you are your doppelganger. Imagine meeting your doppelganger and getting to know them. You are shocked to discover that you both have the same great taste in music. You like the same kinds of movies. You love the same books. You even have the same hobbies!

Wow, this person is great!

You get to know them a bit better.

You discover that they had the same fucked up childhood that you did. They ran into the same types of bullies. They experienced the same kinds of insecurities. Your heart aches for this person, and you just want to tell them it's OK. You want to tell them, "Don't judge yourself!"

Well, that's YOU. Don't judge yourself.

If there's one thing that I've learned from 20+ years as a Neuro Emotional Technique practitioner, it's that all people struggle with their inner critics.

All people feel that they are not good enough.

They all get the feeling that they cannot measure up to other people.

This is just the human condition. It is so universal that it's likely to be a feature, not a bug, formed through evolution to cause us to strive more and more for improvement. No matter how real it *feels*, you just have to work on letting it go.

Ultimately, nobody cares about you. They only care about themselves. It doesn't mean that they are bad people, it's just the way it is! Ultimately, you are just a character in everyone else's movie – just as they are ultimately characters in your movie. Even your cat, who might like you more than anyone else, will eat your face off if you die. (According to a firefighter I know, they will eat your face, but they will not eat your eyeballs.)

When I was in chiropractic school, I become more and more aware of and uncomfortable with the reality of my transgender identity. I thought about the future, and what it would look like if I finally found the courage to transition. In my mind, I thought for certain that I would have to completely change my identity. New name. Shut down my business. Move to another city. Start all over again. Like some fugitive! I didn't know what in the world I would do during the awkward in-between stage. It's not like you take a shot of testosterone and then whammo, you have a full beard, and nobody is the wiser! It was terrifying. I delayed transition for many years.

When it finally happened, and I couldn't live any longer without moving forward, I was terrified of what would happen to my practice. At the time, I was taking care of a lot of Jehovah's Witnesses. I thought, "I'm going to lose all the JWs!" I know, you're wondering, how is it that I, of all people, had a practice full of Jehovah's Witnesses? Well, they tend to be interested in natural methods of healing, and they are great internal networkers. They are a tight knit community basically trained to spread the word.

But a funny thing happened. As I slowly started the roll out and let people know that I was transitioning, almost everyone responded in the same way.

"So, I have something to tell you," I would begin. And the patient would get a concerned look on their face.

"Are you moving?" they would ask.

"No... I'm transitioning to male."

"But you're not moving?"

"No, I'm not moving."

"Oh. OK." And that was pretty much it.

The #1 concern was that I wasn't moving and would still be around to take care of them! Of all my patients, not one of the JWs left on account of my transition (that I am aware of). One of them told me about a conversation she had with her husband about my transition. When she asked her husband what he thought about it, his answer was, "Well, nobody cracks my back like Dr. Kim, so, I guess it's OK with me!"

In fact, the only person who freaked out and left was a gay man! He said that it was just too much change for him, that he couldn't handle it, and that he would not be able to continue as my patient. I was sad and surprised. I had not expected the rejection to come from a fellow member of the rainbow coalition.

That whole rainbow coalition, by the way, does not exist in the way that straight people think it does. There are plenty of Gs and Ls who are not supportive of Bs and Ts, and so on and so forth. The rainbow is a great representation of diversity. But humans are complicated. There is no monolithic group of humans that agrees on everything and loves everyone within even their own special group.

As for that gay man who "couldn't handle" the change? He hurt his back about a year or two later and made an appointment with me out of sheer desperation. When I opened the door for him, he looked at me in surprise and said, "You're... you're still you!"

While I had changed a lot in some ways – a more angular body shape, a bit of stubble on my face, a deeper voice – I was, indeed, still me. He ended up returning as a regular, and we are friends to this day.

People often wonder about how my transition affected my son, who was just 3 years old when I started taking testosterone. The conversation with my 3-year-old son was very much like the conversations with the JWs. I wasn't sure how to say it to such a little kid, but I remember we were in the car, and the conversation went something like this:

"So... I have something important to tell you. I'm going to turn into a boy."

"Well, I don't want to turn into a girl!"

"You're not going to turn into a girl. Only I'm going to change."

"I don't have to turn into a girl?"

"No! You won't turn into a girl. You'll stay a boy. I'll still be your mom, but I'll become a boy. So, just don't call me 'mom' in the men's room."

"Well don't call me Shin in the men's room."

"What should I call you in the men's room??"

"Call me... Lee."

"OK..."

"And don't leave me!"

"I'm not leaving you! I'm not going anywhere."

And finally, he concluded with, "OK well, don't leave me, and love me lots."

And from that day forth, even though he was just 3 years old, he never called me "she" again (though he still calls me mom – because I'm still his mom). It still blows my mind. A 3-year-old could get the gender and pronoun thing down immediately.

Meanwhile, there are still adults – 15 years after my transition – who still insist on calling me "she." What is that about anyway? One uncle recently said to me, "No matter what, you'll always be that 5-year-old little girl to me." I guess that's a whole 'nother topic. The point is, no matter what's going on with you, people care about how it's going to affect *them*. So don't worry about other people and what they might be thinking about. They are not thinking about you. At least not in the way you think they are thinking!

If you ask most people what they think the opposite of love is, they will immediately reply that the opposite of love is hate. But this is not true. The opposite of love is indifference. That's why sometimes even arch enemies get a bit wistful when their nemesis dies. Strong attention is actually a form of love, even if it seems to be very negative. I know, twisted, huh. But indifference really is the opposite of love, just as boredom is the true opposite of happiness.

So, to fall in love with your body, you have to pay attention to it. You can't ignore it, cover it up and hope it will go away!

Become intimately aware of it. Pay attention to it. Look very closely at it. Look at the tiny pores on your skin. While my mom was in acupuncture school, she learned about tongue diagnosis. This is the art of examining the tongue to diagnose problems in the body. She taught the basics to my brother, who started using it first thing in the morning as a daily self-check-in. It sounds weird, but to be honest, you can learn a lot about your body by carefully examining almost any part of it from day to day! You can easily tell if you need better hydration, more vegetables and fruits, more protein, healthy oils...

The body tells all.

The issues are in the tissues!

To love your body and feel comfortable in your skin, you need to take care of your body. Body care includes regular exercise, clean diet, enough sleep and regular supportive body work. I include things like chiropractic, acupuncture, and massage in that body work category. In a perfect world, I recommend doing one of these good "special" things a week. Chiropractic one week, acupuncture one week, a massage one week and so forth. This may not be practical for many people. Do your best. Find your groove. Find what *really* works for you and *your* body.

Meditation and mindfulness are incredibly powerful and can be started with just a few minutes a day. I like to do a short 10-minute meditation first thing in the morning. Pro tip: don't try this laying down. It doesn't work. Another friend used to say that to shine your light in the world, you don't have a be lighthouse beacon. If you don't feel like you have that much energy, you can be a blinky light, like on a bike. Don't worry – people can still see a blinky light from far away!

When you let go of self-judgement, take care of your body, and take in the magic of life, then you will find that at last, you are comfortable in your own skin.

Epilogue

Spoiler Alert! This is IT.

Spoiler alert! This life is your only life.

I know I'll get an earful from lots of people on this one. It can be a terrifying thought. Believing that this life is just a small and insignificant part of our "eternal life" is a comforting thought for a lot of people. The way it was framed for me growing up, though, felt like a big demotivator.

When I would try to share interests or things that I was doing in my life, my mom used to say to me, "Why are you doing that? You can do that when you're dead! Don't waste your time doing things like that. Focus on saving your soul, and once you get into Heaven, you can do all those other things. You can make art when you're dead."

Sorry mom, but you can't make art when you're dead. The older I get, the more dead people I see. The more dead people I see, the more I am convinced that you definitely cannot make art when you're dead. You can BE art when you're dead (hello Body Worlds!) but you cannot MAKE art when you're dead.

Whether you believe in reincarnation, interdimensional realms, Heavens, Hells or just lights out, one fact remains. THIS life, right now, is the only one that YOU, the creature reading this book, has to live. Your experiences and perceptions exist solely through the lens of your body.

Even if there is any "spirit" future beyond this life, it won't have any resemblance to the "you" that is here right now. You won't be "looking down" at your funeral, because you won't have eyeballs anymore. You won't be feeling your feelings because feelings happen through your body. And your body will be out of commission. Other people can tell stories about you, remember you, keep your legacy alive, but as far are YOU are concerned? All you have is the window of time between first consciousness and lights out.

Maybe it's the old goth in me, maybe it's the old Catholic, but for me, death has always been a great motivator. It reminds me that my time is finite and whatever it is that I think is so important, I better focus on it. The older I get, the larger this concept looms. In our current American culture, we are so disconnected from death.

Death is the one thing that is certain for every single one of us, and yet we hide it from view. It's treated as something dirty or clinical. Our people die in hospital settings. If they are lucky, they die at home, but are then taken away as soon as possible. They are not seen again until they are cleaned up for presentation in a casket. Except for at the funeral itself, we rarely even see hearses anymore. Bodies are now transported from the home in white SUVs driven by strong young men in suits. Wouldn't want to attract "negative attention!"

The more comfortable you can get with death – in particular your own death – the richer your life can be, and the more peace of mind you can experience. Also, the more it will help you to focus on your business and what the life of your business means! But not always in the way that you think.

In 2011, Bronnie Ware, an Australian palliative care worker, published a book called *The Top Five Regrets of the Dying*. During her career, she noticed that most dying people have the same regrets. She compiled the top five and here they are:

1. "I wish I'd had the courage to live a life true to myself, not the life others expected of me."

2. "I wish I hadn't worked so hard."

3. "I wish I'd had the courage to express my feelings."

4. "I wish I had stayed in touch with my friends."

5. "I wish that I had let myself be happier."

Number 2 is a really important one, especially for businesspeople and the self-employed. As businesspeople, and for sure as self-employed people, we often work TOO MUCH. It seems really important, and we think, "But this is so that later I will be able to relax!"

But... it doesn't work out that way.

Life is happening in the now. We need boundaries. A couple of years ago, while talking to my son, I asked him, out of curiosity, what the hardest years of his childhood had been. I wondered if it would be the year that I transitioned. I wondered if it would be the year that he had that incredibly shitty 2nd grade teacher. I wondered if it was the year that there was the upheaval of when his grandmother died. Or when he had to move out of the house that he thought he would someday inherit.

No, he named a year that had been completely off my radar.

I was surprised and thought about it... how could I have not noticed that my son was having his hardest year of his life? What was going on in *my* life that had made me oblivious?

My stomach turned when I realized that the year he named as his worst was the year when I was having my "best year ever" in business. My focus was so intensely on my business and what was happening there that I was not very present at all with what was happening in my son's life. I thought that I was doing great and doing great "for him."

But I wasn't.

While I'm glad that I didn't lose even more years in that clueless oblivion, it was still a wake-up call. As I'm writing this, my son is signing up for his freshman college classes, and I feel like, OK, I can focus again on my business!

When I was sitting there in the ER with all those leads coming off my chest, I was thinking about how my heart could quit on me at any time. How I could unceremoniously drop dead on a random Tuesday afternoon. I was not experiencing any of the top five regrets of the dying. I had been conscious of these for years. I often thought about them, making sure to live my life in a way such that I would not have these regrets when my turn rolled around. But I did have a glaring regret.

The regret was that I had not done enough to pass the baton, so speak. I like to think that along the way, I have helped and inspired some other people to live better lives. I thought that therefore, the world could be a little better as that positive momentum spread. But I felt a terrible sense that I had not done nearly enough. I did not leave behind the knowledge that I had gained in my life so that it could help someone in the future!

This book is my baton that I am passing on to whoever cares to take it and run with it. It will certainly outlive me, whether I die next month (that would be awkward) or whether I manage to squeeze out another 40 years! (To be honest, that doesn't sound that great, either. When my grandma turned 92, I was like, "Wow, Gramma! You're 92, that's amazing!" and she said, "It's not that great. All your friends are dead and people treat you like furniture. You feel the same inside, but you look in the mirror and you think, 'MY GOD. What the hell happened to YOU??" So... Anyway...)

There are some great death-positivity books out there. I love Caitlin Doughty's book, *Smoke Gets in Your Eyes: And Other Lessons from the Crematory*. Also, *Die Wise: A Manifesto for Sanity and Soul* by Stephen Jenkinson and *A Beginner's Guide to the End: Practical Advice for Living Life and Facing Death*, by Dr. BJ Miller and Shoshana Berger.

When I thought I was dying back in 2012 (false alarm!) I went and bought my own burial niche at the San Francisco Columbarium. I got a sweet corner niche in the Hall of Dionysus, with a great view of Hermes. It's one of the only places in San Francisco where you can still be interred if you opt for cremation or something like that. You still can't be buried in San Francisco. I like to visit my niche a few times a year, check out my neighbors and all that.

Facing your death can be great for your business. It can help you to back off if you are spending too much time and energy in and on it. But it can also motivate you to get real and laser-focused on what you truly want to accomplish and achieve in your business! Do you need to hire a coach? Do you need to streamline and simplify? Is this business even the business that you want to be doing at all?

Tangentially related to the death topic is the aging topic. As we age, our bodies change. They slow down in a lot of ways. They take longer to heal. The mind is not as sharp as it used to be. As a businessperson making friends with your body and working together, you will want to plan accordingly.

As young people, we often think of "retirement" as just being leisurely old people taking cruises or riding golf carts. But ultimately, we're looking to be able to live a compassionate life for ourselves. It's not about getting to do nothing someday. It's about getting to always live in peace with your body, which naturally means slowing the pace of certain things at a certain time.

In the words of another one of my mentors, the great Dr. Kerby Landis, "Success is an inside job." You have to feel it on the inside before it can manifest on the outside. "Inside" means not just inside your head, but inside your whole body! So, keep on getting comfortable in your own skin. Because when you're in the flow, everything flows – in business and in life.

I am serious about the baton thing! Pass this book on to someone who needs it! What about you? Join us on the next leg of your journey at issuesinthetissuesbook.com